The RAPTURE and REVELATION

The
RAPTURE
and
REVELATION

RAY H. HUGHES

All Scripture quotations are from the King James
Version of the Bible.

Book Editor: Wanda Griffith
Editorial Assistant: Tammy Hatfield
Copy Editor: Oreeda Burnette
Inside Layout: Cresta Shawver

Library of Congress Catalog Card Number: 00-105783
ISBN: 0-87148-745-4

Dedication

To my lovely wife,

Euverla,

*who has fulfilled the Biblical
instruction "to be faithful in all things."
It is especially appropriate for me to
dedicate this book to her because
of her keen interest in prophecy.*

Table of Contents

Foreword

Ray H. Hughes is many things: a Pentecostal Christian, a loving husband, a devoted father, a loyal friend, a true statesman of the church and an international spokesman for the Pentecostal faith and mission. But in this book, we are reminded that he is, at his passionate center, an anointed preacher of the gospel of Jesus Christ. These are not speculative essays debating endtime details. What follows are gospel sermons, which were preached with anointing and passion and meant to persuade men and women to get ready for the coming of the Lord.

Perhaps a few words about eschatology or the last things will serve as a good introduction or preparation for the reading of these sermons. We live in a day in which there is often talk about the end of the world due to atomic explosions, biological warfare, the destruction of the ozone layer with resultant burning up of plant and animal life or the natural emergence of some new virus for which there will be no cure (think of AIDS).

Paradoxically, it is also a time in which men and women often seem to have less fear of God, even in the church. Having eaten of the Tree of Knowledge of Good and Evil and become the arbiters of their own ethical standards, modern 21st century persons have now turned their attention to the Tree of Life. The Human Genome Project will identify the genetic code which programs every cell of the human body and determines all individual human characteristics. Scientists will try to discover a genetic way to extend life, perhaps hundreds of years.

But this will not be the same as eternal life! Only God is eternal. And God has pronounced a death sentence over all creation, while offering life to all through His son Jesus Christ.

In pride and self-assertion, men and women are making plans for the future which often do not include God. But everyone has a view of the end or the ultimate goal of humanity. It is the view of the end that determines our daily planning and makes meaningful our daily activities.

Christians speak of the day the Lord Jesus Christ will appear and all the nations and all the people of the world will be judged. Included in the Christian view of last things are death, the intermediate state, the Rapture, the Millennium, the Tribulation, the Last Judgment, hell, heaven, and so forth. For Christians the end is not some final unrelated point of time beyond which there is nothing. Rather, it is the goal of our life and the limit to all human pride and planning. What you really believe about the end will determine how you actually live. And how you actually live bears witness to what you believe about the end.

Any preaching of the end or the last things should include the following elements:

1. It should be relevant to the present needs of modern men and women.

2. It should be sufficiently futuristic; that is, it should honor the new and wonderful thing that God is going to do at the end for all those who love Him.

3. It should be gospel-centered. Any preaching of hell should be done in the context of the gospel and the

gracious offer of God's love in Jesus Christ. This preaching should be characterized by tears and longing and persuasion.

4. It should be centered on God as the last thing. The Book of Revelation is not primarily about last things; it is primarily about God. God is our hope and our eternal home.

As you read these sermons you will see that they meet these criteria, for Dr. Hughes speaks to the hearts of this present generation while holding to the mystery and wonder of what God has prepared for those who love the appearing of Christ.

These sermons grow out of a gospel perspective that seeks to persuade all persons to be ready for Christ's coming by living holy and being a faithful witness to Christ. Finally, these sermons are centered in God and His plan for a new heaven and a new earth wherein dwells righteousness.

In conclusion, let me offer a response to two common objections to Christian teaching and preaching about last things:

1. The injustice of sentencing someone to eternal torment in hell because of a few temporal sins

2. The prospect of spending an eternity in boredom as one lies on a cloud and strums a harp.

To the first, it must be said that no one will go to hell because he or she has committed three or four or five or six sins. Here we must remind modern men and women that when they practice lying they become liars, when they practice adultery they become adulterers and when they practice murder they become murderers. The Bible never separates the deeds from the doers. God has so ordered human existence that our being is expressed in our doing, and our doing shapes and determines our character. Heaven will be a place of love, truth, and giving and therefore murderers, liars, adulterers, and so forth, will have no place there. In rejecting the will of God, they have rejected God and rejected God's destination for all those who love Him.

To the second objection, heaven will be boring only if God is boring. And God is exceedingly wonderful, possessing infinite wisdom, knowledge, and beauty. The creator of unlimited diversity, exquisite design and profound purpose has prepared a place for us the likes of which no one has ever seen, heard or even imagined!

As you read these sermons I pray that your heart is moved to love and serve God in the beauty of holiness and to be a faithful witness in the light of His soon coming. Let us thank God for Dr. Ray H. Hughes and the gift of this good book.

—Dr. Steven J. Land, Dean
Church of God Theological Seminary

*We which are alive and remain
shall be caught up together with
them in the clouds, to meet the
Lord in the air: and so shall we
ever be with the Lord. Wherefore
comfort one another with these words*
(1 Thessalonians 4:17, 18).

1

The Rapture of the Church

Introduction

The signs of this age indicate we are living in the end time. As we see the day of Christ's return approaching, more and more people are asking, "Will the church go through the Tribulation period? Or, will the saints of God be delivered from it?"

There are several schools of thought concerning the Rapture of the church in relationship to the Tribulation. There is the Partial-Rapture theory which teaches that, when Christ comes, only a portion of the church will go while the balance of lukewarm believers will be left to go through the Tribulation as a period of sanctification. Others proclaim a Post-Tribulation view of the Rapture, believing the church will go through all of the Tribulation period.

Still others believe in a Mid-Tribulation Rapture, that Christ will return during the middle of the Tribulation.

Finally, there are those of us who believe in the Pre-Tribulation Rapture, which teaches that the true church will be caught away to be with the Lord before the Tribulation period.

Although there is a great deal of conflict and confusion on this particular subject, it yet remains a vital and important doctrine. The Coming of the Lord Jesus Christ is the blessed hope of the church. If Satan can confuse us on this particular point, he has won a great victory.

The Meaning of the Rapture

To what are we referring when we speak of the *Rapture?* The word *rapture* is not a Biblical word. Nowhere is it found in the Scriptures. However, it is the best word that we have in the English language to express the well-documented Scriptural view concerning the coming of the Lord Jesus Christ for His church.

The word *rapture* comes from the Latin root *rapio,* which means "to snatch away suddenly."

Jesus told His disciples, "I will come again, and receive you unto myself; that where I am, there ye may be also" (John 14:3).

Paul, writing to the church at Thessalonica, said

> For the Lord himself shall descend from heaven with a shout, with the voice of the archangel, and with the trump of God: and the dead in Christ shall rise first: Then we which are alive and remain shall be caught up together with them in the clouds, to meet the Lord in the air: and so shall we ever be with the Lord (1 Thessalonians 4:16, 17).

Again Paul refers to this event when he prefaces a statement with these words, "Now we beseech you, brethren, by the coming of our Lord Jesus Christ, and by our gathering together unto him" (2 Thessalonians 2:1).

Notice these three phrases:

1. "I will receive you unto myself,"

2. "Caught up together with him in the clouds," and

3. "Our gathering together unto him."

When the dead in Christ are resurrected, the living saints are transformed. Those who are Christ's—those who make up the true church—are translated and caught up to meet Him in the air. This will be the Rapture of the church.

The serious questions are:

1. When will this Rapture take place?

2. Will the saints of God be taken out of the world before the Tribulation period?

3. Will the saints be translated during the Tribulation period? Or,

4. Will the saints go through the entire Tribulation period before they are raptured?

I believe the Bible is clear on this matter, and we need not be in the dark.

Pre-Tribulation Rapture

The concept of a Pre-Tribulation Rapture has long been established among evangelicals and in Pentecostal circles. We believe there is ample Scriptural documentation for our assertion that the church will not go through any part of the

Tribulation period, but will be caught up to meet the Lord in the air before the actual Tribulation period begins.

Nowhere in Scripture is the church associated with the Tribulation period or the time of judgment that shall come upon the earth, called "Daniel's Seventieth Week," or "The Day of Jacob's Trouble."

According to Jeremiah the Tribulation period is a time of judgment for Israel: "Alas! for that day is great, so that none is like it: it is even the time of Jacob's trouble; but he shall be saved out of it" (Jeremiah 30:7).

According to Daniel: "Seventy weeks are determined upon thy people and upon thy holy city" (Daniel 9:24). This passage refers directly to Israel and not to the church. No place in Scripture mentions the church being on earth during the Tribulation period.

Also, we must recognize that the very nature of the Tribulation period argues against the church going through any part of it. The Tribulation period is a time of judgment, a time when the wrath of God is poured out upon the earth. God's church is His purchased possession, and He has saved us from the wrath to come. The church is not looking for the wrath and the judgment of God, but for the blessed hope which is deliverance from the wrath to come.

When writing to the Thessalonians, Paul gives a beautiful description of the Rapture of the church (1 Thessalonians 4:13-18). In the next chapter he continues with this theme of the Lord's Coming, noting,

> But of the times and the seasons, brethren, ye have no need that I write unto you. For yourselves know perfectly that the day of the Lord so cometh as a

thief in the night. For when they shall say, Peace
and safety; then sudden destruction cometh upon
them, as travail upon a woman with child; and they
shall not escape (1 Thessalonians 5:1-3).

For these reasons I am firmly convinced the church
will not be subjected to any portion of what is referred to
in Scripture as the Tribulation period. Of course, this
does not mean the church will not and does not suffer tri-
als and tribulations. These are with us always, even as
Paul told us, "Yea, and all that will live godly in Christ
Jesus shall suffer persecution" (2 Timothy 3:12); but the
saints of God will be caught away and rejoicing with the
Lord when the "sudden destruction," "wrath of God,"
Tribulation period comes upon the world.

The reason I do not believe in a Partial Rapture is that
God's Word says, "But every man in his own order: Christ
the firstfruits; afterward they that are Christ's at his coming"
(1 Corinthians 15:23). Therefore, those who are in Christ,
those who are recognized as Christ's at His coming, they
shall be caught up to meet the Lord in the air.

Saved From Wrath

Paul offers the church consolation, as if to say, "Brethren,
don't worry about the Tribulation period," for he writes,

But ye, brethren, are not in darkness, that that day
should overtake you as a thief. Ye are all the children of light, and the children of the day: we are
not of the night, nor of darkness. Therefore let us
not sleep, as do others; but let us watch and be
sober (1 Thessalonians 5:4-6).

Again he writes, "For God hath not appointed us to wrath, but to obtain salvation by our Lord Jesus Christ, Who died for us, that, whether we wake or sleep, we should live together with him" (1 Thessalonians 5:9, 10). Highlight the phrase, *God has not appointed us to wrath.* Paul is talking to the church, to the believers at Thessalonica, the children of light. The saints are appointed *to obtain salvation by our Lord Jesus Christ.* The word *salvation* in this verse does not mean the forgiveness of sins only, but it carries with it the same meaning as in the Book of Hebrews "And unto them that look for him shall he appear the second time without sin unto salvation" (Hebrews 9:28). It is the full and total *salvation* of the saints—spirit, soul and body—or, the catching away of the saints to meet the Lord in the air.

This understanding is verified by the context, for the next verse says, "Who died for us, that, whether we wake or sleep, we should live together with him" (1 Thessalonians 5:10).

Other references supporting this understanding are:

> And to wait for his Son from heaven, whom he raised from the dead, even Jesus, which delivered us from the wrath to come (1 Thessalonians 1:10).

> And to you who are troubled rest with us, when the Lord Jesus shall be revealed from heaven with his mighty angels, In flaming fire taking vengeance on them that know not God, and that obey not the gospel of our Lord Jesus Christ: Who shall be punished with everlasting destruction from the presence of the Lord, and from the glory of his power (2 Thessalonians 1:7- 9).

The phrase, *to you who are troubled rest with us,* deserves special attention. While the rest of the world shall receive the torrents of God's flaming judgment, the saints will be at rest with Him. This has always been the principle of God's operation.

God did not destroy the first world until Noah was safe in the ark and God had shut him in. He said to Noah, "Come thou and all thy house into the ark" (Genesis 7:1). "And the Lord shut him in" (v. 16).

God did not destroy Sodom and Gomorrah until righteous Lot was delivered.

And not until the church is raptured from the world will God pour His judgment upon this earth. The church age is a day of grace, a time of mercy and longsuffering. God did not tell us that He would preserve the church in the Tribulation period, nor that He would preserve the church through the hours of judgment. But He did say, "Watch ye therefore, and pray always, that ye may be accounted worthy to escape all these things that shall come to pass, and to stand before the Son of man" (Luke 21:36).

Thus, as God's children, we take courage and hope in knowing that God's love, already expressed in the giving of His beloved Son on a cross, will be expressed once again when He raptures away the church in order that we not suffer the awful things coming upon our world.

The Church in Heaven

In the Book of Revelation, after the saints have been raptured, the church is not again pictured upon the earth. From chapters 4 through 19, the church is seen in heaven around the throne eternal, robed in linen clean and white, with crowns of gold upon their heads, then coming back with Jesus Christ who will defeat the Antichrist and establish the kingdom of the Lord Jesus Christ upon the earth.

Before the fourth chapter of the Revelation, the church is mentioned 14 times. Each time it is the church on the earth. Beginning with the fourth chapter, the church is caught up, and God no longer deals with the church on earth, but the church (the redeemed of the Lord) in heaven.

Further conclusive proof of the Pre-Tribulation Rapture is found in the Second Book of Thessalonians.

Since the two books of Thessalonians are devoted entirely to the subject of the coming of the Lord, they are called Books of the Advent. The apostle Paul had written the First Book of Thessalonians describing the Rapture, or the coming of the Lord, for the church. During the interval between Paul's first and second epistles, some false prophet had written a letter, forging Paul's name, and stating the Tribulation had already come. He said the persecution through which the church was going at the moment was the Tribulation period.

The saints at Thessalonica had become quite disturbed. They knew the apostle Paul had said they would be delivered—the Rapture would take place *before* the wrath. Thus, Paul's second letter to the church at Thessalonica became necessary.

These were his opening words in chapter two:

> Now we beseech you, brethren, by the coming of
> our Lord Jesus Christ, and by our gathering togeth-
> er unto him, That ye be not soon shaken in mind,
> or be troubled, neither by spirit, nor by word, nor
> by letter as from us, as that the day of Christ is at

hand. Let no man deceive you by any means: for that day shall not come, except there come a falling away first, and that man of sin be revealed, the son of perdition; Who opposeth and exalteth himself above all that is called God, or that is worshipped; so that he as God sitteth in the temple of God, shewing himself that he is God. Remember ye not, that, when I was yet with you, I told you these things? And now ye know what withholdeth that he might be revealed in his time. For the mystery of iniquity doth already work: only he who now letteth will let, until he be taken out of the way. And then shall that Wicked be revealed, whom the Lord shall consume with the spirit of his mouth, and shall destroy with the brightness of his coming (2 Thessalonians 2:1-8).

Paul warned the saints they were not to be deceived *by any means*, neither *by spirit* nor *by word*, nor *by an epistle*." He said *that day* shall not come except there be a great apostasy or an abandonment of the faith and the man of sin—the son of perdition, who is the Antichrist—be revealed. This revelation of the Antichrist cannot happen until He who now hinders be taken out of the way. When this hindrance is removed, then the Antichrist shall arise.

The Restraining Forces

This is what Paul is saying: The Tribulation period cannot come, neither can the Antichrist be revealed, until the restraining force—which is the church—is caught up to meet Christ. Therefore, as the body of Christ we need not be looking for wrath, judgment and God's fury to be poured upon the earth; but rather, we need to lift up our heads and rejoice, for our redemption draws nigh.

We need not look for the Tribulation period, but for the Rapture. If the devil can get the church looking for the Tribulation period rather than the Rapture, he will destroy the blessedness of our experience and hope. This is the enemy, Satan, who hates the doctrine of the imminent return of the Lord Jesus Christ. By *imminent return*, I mean that He could come at any moment. There is no sign that needs to be fulfilled before the return of the Lord Jesus Christ. He can come for His church today and do no violence to the Holy Scriptures. If He is not to come until the middle of the Tribulation period or until the end of the Tribulation period, then there is no reason for the church to look for Him until the Tribulation period begins.

Such thinking destroys the glorious hope and constant expectancy of the imminent return of our Lord. Thank God, because the Word says, "Therefore be ye also ready: for in such an hour as ye think not the Son of man cometh" (Matthew 24:44).

Conclusion

Therefore, let us prepare our hearts for the glorious, gladsome event! The Rapture could take place at any moment!

Over the years I have known some who spoke of, and viewed, the Rapture as something of a dreaded event. This should not be true for the believer and it is not in keeping with Scripture. Paul tells us to "comfort one another with these words." We take no pleasure in those unfortunate things which are going to come upon the world. We are not haughty or gleeful. But we are reassured and comforted just to know that our Lord's appearing will bring our deliverance. Thus, we keep our lamps trimmed and burning. We keep our souls tuned to the Holy Spirit. We keep our spiritual eyes turned heavenward, from whence cometh our hope.

If you are not prepared and ready—your sins forgiven, your heart at peace—then I invite you to join me in prayer at this very moment. God is ready to help you.

Let us pray.

> *Dear God, draw near in loving mercy. Touch our hearts anew with the breath of Your Holy Spirit. Renew within us the joy of Your salvation. Give us the strength and the determination to work while it is day, knowing the night soon comes. Help us to commit all things into Your loving arms. Grant us peace. Give us comfort, as we wait for the sounding of the trumpet and our Lord's triumphal return. Amen.*

*But I would not have you to be ignorant,
brethren, concerning them which are asleep,
that ye sorrow not, even as others which
have no hope. For if we believe that Jesus
died and rose again, even so them also which
sleep in Jesus will God bring with him.
For this we say unto you by the word of
the Lord, that we which are alive and remain
unto the coming of the Lord shall not prevent
them which are asleep. For the Lord
himself shall descend from heaven with
a shout, with the voice of the archangel,
and with the trump of God: and the dead
in Christ shall rise first: Then we which
are alive and remain shall be caught up
together with them in the clouds, to meet
the Lord in the air: and so shall we ever be
with the Lord. Wherefore comfort one
another with these words*
(1 Thessalonians 4:13-18).

2

When Jesus Christ Returns

Introduction

The books of 1 and 2 Thessalonians are regarded as Books of the Advent. Here the apostle Paul devotes two entire letters to the doctrine of the Lord's coming and the events connected with it. There is much ignorance in the world concerning the afterlife of man. Some things we cannot understand. However, it is not the will of God that we be ignorant concerning those who are dead and what their future shall be.

In the words of the above text, the apostle Paul exhorts the Thessalonians that there is no need for inordinate sorrow over the death of our loved ones. Such open displays of grief leaves the appearance that we have no hope. The *hope* Christians have in the coming of the Lord Jesus Christ more than makes up for the sorrow and woe that naturally accompanies the death of our Christian loved ones. For this reason we *sorrow not even as others which have no hope.*

The Innate Knowledge of Man

Most religions espouse some form of belief in an afterlife. American Indians believe their afterlife is to be a happy hunting ground. For this reason, they bury the bow and arrow, or other hunting instruments with the dead so they may hunt in the new world. Egyptians built pyramids for their kings, the pharaohs, and buried them with their precious jewels for use in the next life. The Hindu believes in the transmigration of souls. When one dies, he returns in another form, determined by whether he has been good or evil. The philosophy of the Greeks sets forth that humankind will eventually evolve into a perfect society known as a utopia.

The point to be made here is that the very spirit of man, something within each of us, affirms that there must be *life beyond this life.* Even with this innate knowledge, this grain of truth placed within the con-sciousness of man, many yet have not found the real truth. They are ignorant of God's plan of redemption and salvation. They know nothing of the Christian hope.

When Job was being sorely tempted by the devil, he voiced the human cynicism, "Man that is born of a woman is of few days, and full of trouble. He cometh forth like a flower, and is cut down: he fleeth also as a shadow, and continueth not" (Job 14:1, 2).

Job was a sick man. His body was wasting away. The skin worms were eating his flesh. His kinsfolk had failed him, and his close friends had forgotten him. The maids of his house counted him a stranger, an alien in their sight. His servants failed to obey his voice. His own wife turned against him and he agreed with her that he was nigh unto death.

Yet, in his despair, when it seemed there was no hope, Job reasoned thus,

> For there is hope of a tree, if it be cut down, that it will sprout again, and that the tender branch thereof will not cease. Though the root thereof wax old in the earth, and the stock thereof die in the ground; Yet through the scent of water it will bud, and bring forth boughs like a plant. But man dieth, and wasteth away: yea, man giveth up the ghost, and where is he? (vv. 7-10).

Job found a faint hope knowing that if a tree that was cut down could sprout again, perhaps man who died could be raised up as well. Because of this, he asked, "If a man die, shall he live again? all the days of my appointed time will I wait, till my change come" (v. 14).

With this soul searching, and thorough revelation from the God of heaven, Job became convinced about the afterlife. His conviction caused him to cry out,

> Oh that my words were now written! oh that they were printed in a book! That they were graven with an iron pen and lead in the rock forever! For I know that my redeemer liveth, and that he shall stand at the latter day upon the earth: And though after my skin worms destroy this body, yet in my flesh shall I see God (vv. 23-26).

Job was so certain there was life for him beyond this life that he wanted a book of his words published. He wanted not merely an inscription with quill upon a scroll—that could be destroyed—but he desired something written in a manner that generations to come might read and share the truth of his revelation. He cried out for someone to take an iron pen and write his message in a rock that it might last forever. He knew his Kinsman Redeemer was alive. He is not the God of the dead but of the living.

Job came to understand the blessed hope of the saints, the same hope Paul would write about centuries later when he penned the words, "If in this life only we have hope in Christ, we are of all men most miserable" (1 Corinthians 15:19).

God's Revealed Message of Life

Those who are children of God need not despair concerning the future. Death does not annihilate us. Death to the child of God is but undisturbed peace and rest. Dead saints are resting in Christ, under His special care. They have been removed out of this world into a better one. Paul wrote that death is, "to be absent from the body, and to be present with the Lord" (2 Corinthians 5:8). To the Philippians he wrote, "For to me to live is Christ, and to die is gain" (Philippians 1:21).

These passages shed further light on Old Testament passages such as, "Then shall the dust return to the earth as it was: and the spirit shall return unto God who gave it" (Ecclesiastes 12:7); and, "Who knoweth the spirit of man that goeth upward, and the spirit of the beast that goeth downward to the earth?" (Ecclesiastes 3:21).

Our hope hinges on our faith. If we believe that Jesus died and rose again from the dead, then we know that those who are at rest in Jesus will God bring with Him. When the Bible speaks of being asleep in Jesus, it does not mean that the soul of man sleeps. The soul of man is immortal and goes to be with the Lord at death. The bodies of the saints rest in the grave until the morning of the first resurrection. When Jesus breaks the morning and makes His appearance in the clouds, the spirits of the saints of God which are in paradise shall also come forth and enter into the bodies that are in the graves. Then shall the corruptible put on incorruption; the mortal shall put on immortality; weakness shall put on power; and dishonor shall be raised in glory.

This message of the coming of Christ is not the mere product of man's thinking: it is the revealed Word of the Lord. The apostle Paul stated plainly that what he had to say about the coming of the Lord was a divine message, "This we say unto you by the word of the Lord" (1 Thessalonians 4:15). The apostle Peter also declared, "For we have not followed cunningly devised fables, when we made known unto you the power and coming of our Lord Jesus Christ, but were eye witnesses of his majesty" (2 Peter 1:16).

Peter, James and John, bosom disciples of the Lord Jesus Christ, went aside into a high mountain with Christ. Christ was transfigured before them. His face shone as the sun. His raiment became white as the snow—whiter than any fuller's soap could make it. A bright cloud overshadowed Him. On one side of Christ was Moses and on the other Elijah.

The cloud that overshadowed Jesus Christ was typical of His second coming in the clouds of heaven. The presence of Elijah with Christ was typical of the translated saints, for Elijah went to heaven in a whirlwind, not having passed through the natural channel of death. The presence of Moses with Christ was typical of the resurrected saints, for Moses, having been buried by God on Mount Nebo's hillside, appeared in a recognizable form to Peter, James and John.

This is a beautiful picture of Christ's coming in mid air, and the translated and resurrected saints being caught up to meet Him. This occasion was so blessed to the apostle Peter that he wanted to build a tabernacle to honor the three—Christ, Moses and Elijah.

Peter would later discover it was not more churches or tabernacles that were needed, but more of Christ in the church, a truth we need to realize as well.

The Living and the Dead

Those who are alive at the coming of the Lord shall not go before those who are in their graves. Those who are alive and remain shall be caught up together with those who are resurrected from the dead. This is the meaning of the phrase, "shall not prevent them which are asleep" (1 Thessalonians 4:15). The living shall not go *before* or be *caught up before* those who are dead.

Analysis of the previous verses serves as an introduction to what will happen when Jesus comes. This passage was given especially to comfort those early saints in reference to their loved ones who had lived in hope of, but failed to witness, the return of Christ. The reward for the believer is the same whether we go by way of the grave or by way of the Rapture.

The Lord Himself

Paul emphasized, and every believer should rejoice

WHEN JESUS CHRIST RETURNS

and find comfort in, the phrase *The Lord Himself.* Not another savior, not an angel, not a new prophet . . . but the Lord himself will return for His saints. This was also the message of the angel which appeared to the disciples shortly after the resurrection, at the time of the Lord's ascension, "Ye men of Galilee, why stand ye gazing up into heaven? this same Jesus, which is taken up from you into heaven, shall so come in like manner as ye have seen him go into heaven" (Acts 1:11). The same Christ who walked among men, gave Himself on Calvary and came forth out of the borrowed tomb shall come again.

Let us also take note of some further specifics relating to His coming.

1. *With a shout.* Our Lord's second appearing shall be with a shout. His first advent was one of humiliation, poverty and lowly estate. His second appearing is to be one of grandeur and glory. He will come with pomp and power. When He appears, He shall give forth a shout which will be a cry of incitement, an order, a command. His will be a shout of authority, that of a mighty king and conqueror. The Captain of our salvation who has the keys of death and of hell shall give His command.

The Word of God does not tell us precisely what He shall say when He gives this order from the clouds, but we do have a record of what He said to John on the Isle of Patmos. I believe these words may well correspond with what our Master shall say when He shouts from the clouds—"Come up hither, and I will shew thee things which must be hereafter" (Revelation 4:1).

Only those who are Christians will hear this shout or command of Christ. He tells us in John, "My sheep hear my voice, and I know them, and they follow me" (John 10:27). Those who have not heard His voice of pardon and forgiveness will not understand His shout on the day of His coming.

The voice of this conqueror of glory shall even penetrate the graves, and the dead in Christ shall hear His voice. It is not the voice of a victim, but the voice of a victor who has gotten victory over death, hell and the grave:

> Marvel not at this: for the hour is coming, in the which all that are in the graves shall hear his voice, And shall come forth; they that have done good, unto the resurrection of life; and they that have done evil, unto the resurrection of damnation (John 5:28, 29).

Reverend M.G. McLuhan, a minister friend of mine, told me the following story.

The McLuhans lived on a ranch in Western Canada. One day M.G.'s father invited him to go with him to get his sheep from land leased from the government. They arrived at their destination and found 18,000 grazing sheep. Since only 126 of these sheep belonged to his father, M.G. couldn't help but wonder how his father would know which sheep were his.

He watched with fascination as his father walked around the edges of the mass of sheep and shouted forth his own peculiar sheep call. First one, then another, then small groups, until finally, out of that group of 18,000 came marching the 126 blacklegged sheep that lined up and began following their shepherd. They knew the voice of their shepherd. They would not follow another.

Hearing Reverend McLuhan relate that story, I immediately thought of the day when the Chief Shepherd shall appear and give His own peculiar call. His sheep shall hear His voice and shall follow Him up into the clouds of glory. We shall be caught away, raptured away, and so shall we ever be with the Lord. He is coming *with a shout,* His own special voice.

2. *With the voice of the archangel.* After the shout of Christ in the heavens, another voice shall ring from corridor to corridor in glory—the voice of the archangel. Angels accompanied the first appearing of Jesus Christ and sang His welcome song to the earth. At His second appearing, one of the chief angels of glory shall cry forth a sound of victory.

Just what this angel shall say is not certain, but I believe it shall be something like this: "Alleluia: for the Lord God omnipotent reigneth. Let us be glad and rejoice, and give honour to him: for the marriage of the Lamb is come, and his wife hath made herself ready" (Revelation 19:6, 7). The Lord is called the Lord of Sabaoth, which means the Lord of Hosts, and no doubt, this angel will be a general in this host, giving notice to the Christians of the approach of their Redeemer.

In 1952, I was privileged to attend the Pentecostal World Conference in Paris, France. Delegates from 32 different nations gathered to share faith and I soon realized that the one common word, understood by all, was "hallelujah." The word means "Praise ye the Lord." We shared that praise across language and cultural barriers and it was magnificent. I think it would be most appropriate for the angel to introduce Christ at His second coming with a grand and glorious "hallelujah."

3. *With the trump of God.* Some believe the reason for the trumpet blast is to awaken those who are asleep in their graves and to prepare them for the summons of Christ. The Bible gives a very interesting account of the use of trumpets in the activities of Israel.

Through Moses, God instructed,

> Make thee two trumpets of silver; of a whole piece shalt thou make them: that thou mayest use them for the calling of the assembly, and for the journeying of the camps. And when they shall blow with them, all the assembly shall assemble themselves to thee at the door of the tabernacle of the congregation (Numbers 10:2, 3).

One trumpet was to be blown for gathering together of the people, the other was to be blown for the journeying of the camps.

Since the Bible speaks of the last trump, I believe there must be at least two trumpet blasts at the appearing of Christ. The first trumpet blast shall assemble the living and dead together, and the second blast shall be the order for our march to the skies.

4. *With dead saints first.* In response to the command of Christ, the voice of the archangel and the trump of God, the dead in Christ shall rise first. Jesus Christ was firstfruits of the first resurrection when He came forth from the bowels of the earth with the saints of God and led them to paradise, which is above. Paul tells us, "Every man in his own order: Christ the firstfruits; afterward they that are Christ's at his coming" (1 Corinthians 15:23). The first concern of Christ will be His dead saints. He will raise them from the dead before those

who are alive are changed. Those who rest in death will have no less joy than those who do not die.

An age long question has been, "How are the dead raised up? and with what body do they come?" (1 Corinthians 15:35). This was a question in Paul's day. This should not be a matter of too much concern to God's children, for if God reached down into the clay of the earth and formed man and breathed into him the breath of life and he became a living soul, God certainly can bring man forth on the morning of the resurrection. Jesus Christ told the Pharisees, who were attendants at the baptism of John, "God is able of these stones to raise up children unto Abraham" (Matthew 3:9). God shall give each of us, His saints, bodies fit for heaven.

5. *With transformation.* At the Rapture, those who are alive will undergo an instant change, similar to, equivalent to, that which happens at death. How this change will take place, we do not know. It is a mystery yet to be unveiled. This we do know—these mortal bodies shall put on immortality and be made fit to inherit the kingdom of God. The change shall take place "in a moment, in the twinkling of an eye" (1 Corinthians 15:52). The saints of God shall shed their mortal, decaying bodies and shall receive new bodies that are not subject to the powers of sin and sickness. We shall become as Christ and be counted worthy of another world,

> For our conversation is in heaven; from whence also we look for the Saviour, the Lord Jesus Christ: Who shall change our vile body, that it may be fashioned like unto his glorious body, according to the working whereby he is able even to subdue all things unto himself (Philippians 3:20, 21).

Thus can we say with Job, "All the days of my appointed time will I wait, till my change come" (14:14). This is the hope of every child of God.

6. *With translation.* Both those brought forth from the dead and those who are changed shall meet together in the clouds and there be joined with the Lord in the air. This catching away to meet Christ in the air is called the *rapture* of the church. It is a gathering together unto Him who purchased the church. For when He comes, the saints shall receive a crown of glory and shall ever be with the Lord. This translation means constant companionship with the Lord Jesus Christ throughout eternity. With these words, the saints of God should comfort each other.

The apostle Paul used the message of the coming of the Lord to beseech and entreat the saints to better living and stability:

> Now we beseech you, brethren, by the coming of
> our Lord Jesus Christ, and by our gathering togeth-
> er unto him, That ye be not soon shaken in mind, or
> be troubled, neither by spirit, nor by word, nor by
> letter as from us, as that the day of Christ is at hand
> (2 Thessalonians 2:1, 2).

In summary, Jesus himself shall descend from heaven with an order or command, beckoning the children of God to the skies. The archangel shall cry forth, announcing Christ's coming. Trumpet blasts shall resound across the universe. The spirits of the departed saints shall enter into their bodies, and the graves shall burst forth. The first resurrection will have taken place.

At the same moment, mysteriously, the living saints shall be changed from mortal to immortal beings. The power of the Holy Spirit shall overcome the power of gravity. Together, they shall be caught up in the clouds to meet the Lord in the air.

What a blessed thought this is to the children of God!

The Plight of the Sinner

While the coming of the Lord Jesus Christ is the blessed hope of the church, the same is not true for the sinner. The Lord's return in power and judgment is, or should be, the constant dread of the sinner. How terrible that moment will be for those unprepared to meet God.

I have often thought of the description of the new heaven and the new earth given to John the Revelator on the Isle of Patmos. In the midst of his vision, the horrible fate of the sinner was described,

> But the fearful, and unbelieving, and the abominable, and murderers, and whoremongers, and sorcerers, and idolaters, and all liars, shall have their part in the lake which burneth with fire and brimstone: which is the second death (Revelation 21:8).

This is the inevitable destiny of those who will not prepare for this joyous event of the saints. The sinner will be left on earth to face the loss of loved ones. He will be tormented by a guilty conscience for having rejected Christ. He will be subjected to all the horrors and terrors of the Tribulation period, during which time there shall be a great earthquakes and natural upheavals beyond any known on this earth before.

The sun shall become black as sackcloth of hair. The moon shall become as blood. The stars of heaven shall fall.

The heavens themselves shall depart and roll together. Mountains and islands shall move out of their places.

> And the kings of the earth, and the great men, and the rich men, and the chief captains, and the mighty men, and every bondman, and every free man, hid themselves in the dens and in the rocks of the mountains; And said to the mountains and rocks, Fall on us, and hide us from the face of him that sitteth on the throne, and from the wrath of the Lamb: For the great day of his wrath is come; and who shall be able to stand? (Revelation 6:15-17).

Those left upon this earth shall also be subjected to the vials of the wrath of God that will be poured out. Men will not be able to buy or sell without the mark of the Antichrist upon them. If they receive this mark, a noisome, grievous sore shall come upon them. The sea shall become as blood, and every living soul in the sea shall die. The fountains of water and rivers shall become blood. The sun at one period shall become so hot that it will scorch men with its heat. Men shall blaspheme the name of God but repent not.

The kingdom of the Antichrist shall become full of darkness, and men will gnaw their tongues for pain. It will be a time of unrestrained activity of evil spirits and spirits of devils working miracles. The earth will quake. Islands shall flee away. Mountains shall not be found, and hail shall fall from heaven upon men.

These judgments and many others shall rain down like water upon the wicked. Finally, the wicked shall come to the judgment bar of God and give an account of themselves for their wicked deeds and they shall be cast into the lake of fire to burn forever and ever.

Conclusion

Such need not happen to you. God has provided salvation for all who will believe in the name of His Son Jesus Christ. God loved you so much He sent His Son to die in your place, for your sins, that you might be delivered from the wrath to come. Acknowledge your sinful rebellion at this very moment. Confess your sins. Ask God for forgiveness. Welcome Jesus Christ as Lord of your life.

That's how simple it is, "There is none other name under heaven given among men, whereby we must be saved" (Acts 4:12); and I invite you to pray with me at this moment.

> *Father in heaven, with humble hearts we acknowledge You as Creator of heaven and earth. We accept Your Son Jesus into our hearts. We proclaim Him Lord of all. We seek grace and mercy, as provided on the cross of Calvary, and we affirm our love and determination to serve You all the days of our life. Hear us, Oh God. Forgive us. Keep us safely in Your arms of love, for thine is the Kingdom, the power, and the glory, forever. Amen.*

And they worshipped the beast, saying,
Who is like unto the beast? who is able to
make war with him? And there was given
unto him a mouth speaking great things and
blasphemies; and power was given unto him
to continue forty and two months. And he
opened his mouth in blasphemy against
God, to blaspheme his name, and his
tabernacle, and them that dwell in heaven.
And it was given unto him to make war
with the saints, and to overcome them:
and power was given him over all kindreds,
and tongues, and nations. And all that
dwell upon the earth shall worship him,
whose names are not written in the book
of life of the Lamb slain from
the foundation of the world
(Revelation 13:4-8).

3

The Rise of the Antichrist

Introduction

There is an event immediately after the Rapture called "The Rise of The Antichrist." Contrary to the belief of many people, the coming of Christ for His saints is not the end of the world. The existence of the church in the world is the only thing that has kept this world from becoming completely corrupt and depraved. When the church departs this world, unrestrained lawlessness will be rampant in the land.

The Bible plainly teaches that the Antichrist will be revealed after the rapture of the church. Paul, writing to the Thessalonians, refers to the mystery of iniquity and the grace of God that keeps iniquity in check (2 Thessalonians 2:7). He goes on to write, "Then shall that Wicked be revealed, whom the Lord shall consume with the spirit of his mouth, and shall destroy with the brightness of his coming" (v. 8).

The Antichrist will arise at a time when the world is confused, frustrated and horror-stricken. It will be a time when people will be easily susceptible to any power that will promise peace.

The Person of the Antichrist

With new schemes, plans and inventions, the Antichrist will proceed to reconstruct the patterns of society. The world will have just experienced the shock of missing loved ones and disappearing friends. Disorder will prevail throughout the business, social and governmental structures of the world and all of humanity. Those left behind in the wake of the Rapture, will be desperately seeking for a solution to the turmoil and chaos.

Against that backdrop, a new and charming statesman will suddenly appear on the scene. He will show great resource, extraordinary skill and smooth diplomacy. Inspired of Satan himself, the Antichrist will display a previously unknown ability to coordinate, lead and persuade the powers of the world. He will bring those powers into a federation for mutual protection, mutual strength and mutual economic partnership. He will promise peace and order for the entire world, and the people of the world will believe him.

One of the most persistent cries of the human heart has always been for peace. Ever since Satan disturbed the peace of humankind in the Garden of Eden, there has been a yearning for a return to that paradise. Men have sought for peace everywhere and in everything, not realizing that Christ Jesus himself is the only source of real peace. He is correctly named the Prince of Peace.

Through his political claims and boasts, the Antichrist will gain universal support, so much so that very shortly the power of supreme dictatorship will be vested in him. He will become the imperial head of the revived Roman Empire, and all the world will wonder about him (Revelation 13).

The Power of the Antichrist

Because his promises are so captivating, men all over the world will rejoice and give support to this great emperor, the Antichrist. This will be especially true of Israel, for they shall see the Antichrist as a true savior. People will attribute wisdom and greatness to the Antichrist, not realizing that it is really Satan who has given him the power.

Note these Scriptures:

> Even him, whose coming is after the working of Satan with all power and signs and lying wonders, and with all deceivableness of unrighteousness in them that perish; because they receive not the love of the truth, that they might be saved (2 Thessalonians 2:9, 10).

> And the beast which I saw was like unto a leopard, and his feet were as the feet of a bear, and his mouth as the mouth of a lion: and the dragon gave him his power, and his seat, and great authority (Revelation 13:2).

The same Satan that offered Jesus Christ the kingdoms of the world during His temptation in Matthew 4 has now found a willing subject to carry out his bidding.

Let us note some of the other names used in reference to the Antichrist: Writing to the Thessalonians, Paul speaks of *the son of perdition*, and *the lawless one*. In the Book of Revelation, John calls him *the beast*. This same writer refers to him in his first epistle as *the antichrist* (1 John 2:18).

But whatever the designated name, the Antichrist's display of wisdom and ingenuity will soon bring peace out of chaos. With the years, mankind has become so materially minded and so interested in physical ease that they will declare once again that the world has rest and security. All this prosperity will be according to the prophetic words of Daniel. "And through his policy also he shall cause craft to prosper in his hand; and he shall magnify himself in his heart, and by peace shall destroy many; he shall also stand up against the Prince of princes" (Daniel 8:25).

Give close attention to these words, because these are all things to which you will be subjected if you are not ready to meet Jesus Christ when He comes.

The Political Base of the Antichrist

The ten horns of the beast mentioned in Revelation represent the Roman Empire or a league of ten nations (Revelation 13:1). This political entity will be a grand federation of the leading powers of the world, a concert of nations, an earthly kingdom from which the Antichrist shall arise and through which he will exert power over the nations of the world.

> The fourth beast shall be the fourth kingdom upon the earth, which shall be diverse from all kingdoms, and shall devour the whole earth, and shall tread it down, and break it in pieces. The ten horns out of this kingdom are ten kings that shall arise: and another shall rise after them; and he shall be diverse from the first, and he shall subdue three kings (Daniel 7:23, 24).

In light of this fact, I have watched with intense interest the forming of various leagues and federations of nations in recent years. I believe these are forerunners to the final drama of human history soon to be played out upon this earth.

The Pact with Israel

The Antichrist will make a seven-year covenant with Israel. He will deceive the Jews at first and pose as their friend.

Jesus clearly prophesied that His people, the Jews, would accept the Antichrist. "I am come in my Father's name, and ye receive me not: if another shall come in his own name, him ye will receive" (John 5:43). Daniel also prophesied of this event, "He shall confirm the covenant with many for one week" (Daniel 9:27).

The Antichrist will give the Jews a long-yearned-for promise of peace in their ancient land. He will make a covenant that will protect them from all their enemies in the land of Palestine, provided they will give him their allegiance.

For the first three-and-a-half years of this period, things will go well and according to schedule. Then, suddenly, everything will change and the true nature of the Antichrist will be revealed.

With all this new power and authority, and in keeping with his concept of a new world order, the Antichrist will proceed to exalt himself. He will even proclaim himself as God: "Who opposeth and exalteth himself above all that is called God, or that is worshipped; so that he as God sitteth in the temple of God, shewing himself that he is God" (2 Thessalonians 2:5). The Bible indicates that virtually the whole world gives worship to the Antichrist: "And they worshipped the beast, saying, Who is like unto the beast? who is able to make war with him?" (Revelation 13:4).

The Break with Israel

Satan, of course, is not satisfied with the whole world worshiping. He wants more; and, through the Antichrist, wants to be worshiped in a newly rebuilt Jewish temple in Jerusalem. Thus, the Antichrist shall go forth and take possession of the Temple. He shall take his seat in the Holy of Holies, and he shall be a visible god and worshiped as divine.

This event is what Jesus refers to when He said, "When ye therefore shall see the abomination of desolation, spoken of by Daniel the prophet, stand in the holy place (whoso readeth, let him understand)" (Matthew 24:15).

The abomination of desolation is the assumption of deity by the Antichrist when he stops the temple sacrifices and sets up himself as God and demands that the people worship him.

When this event occurs, the Jews will realize they have been deceived. They will resist the Antichrist, but it will be too late. Daniel prophesied many years ago, "In the midst of the week" [in the middle of the tribulation period] "he shall cause the sacrifice and the oblation to cease" (Daniel 9:27).

The False Prophet

The people of the world will worship the Antichrist because of miracles, signs and wonders. Where there is a new religion or a new doctrine, there must be also a false prophet to propound it. What his name will be, what the world will know him by, I do not know, but the title Scripture gives him is "false prophet."

This false prophet is a preacher of this new religion. He is determined that the whole world will have but one religion. The doctrines he espouses are simple and definite:

- Christ is to be renounced

- The authority of Antichrist, the great world ruler, is to be acknowledged and

- The religion of the False Prophet is to become the norm.

The Bible tells us that this false prophet will speak as a dragon. The word *dragon* in the Book of Revelation means *the devil*. So he will be prompted by the devil. The False Prophet will do great wonders and call fire down upon the earth in the sight of all men. He will deceive people that dwell on the earth by means of the miracles which he will have power to do in the sight of the Beast. He will be so persuasive the people will prepare a metallic image of the Beast, and the False Prophet will gather the people together for the dedication of this image (Revelation 13:13-16).

Upon this special occasion, the false prophet will declare that the image itself shall speak. "And he had power to give life unto the image of the beast, that the image of the beast should both speak, and cause that as many as would not worship the image of the beast should be killed" (v. 15).

Men have made tremendous scientific discoveries in our day, but one thing man has not been able to do is to make inanimate objects talk. Nonetheless, the False Prophet will claim to give life to the image and make him speak.

On the day set, the multitudes will be gathered together. When the metallic beast begins to move his lips and speak forth words, the people's hearts will beat wildly and they will fall down to worship him, or be killed.

The Mark of the Beast

In order to further enforce worship in compliance to the Antichrist's decrees, all of the people will be commanded to display a mark upon their foreheads or in the palms of their hands, an open avowal of allegiance or acknowledgment of their worship.

No one will be able to buy or sell unless the mark of the Beast is displayed. Refusal to accept the mark of the Antichrist will bring immediate vengeance.

> And he causeth all, both small and great, rich and poor, free and bond, to receive a mark in their right hand, or in their foreheads: And that no man might buy or sell, save he that had the mark, or the name of the beast, or the number of his name (Revelation 13:16, 17).

All those who receive the mark of the Beast will be committing the unpardonable sin. From that moment, on there will be no chance of repentance or recovery.

All those who will not receive the mark of the Beast will be killed, or else they will be unable to buy or sell goods and perish from starvation.

It is a graphic and terrible picture. When a shopper goes to the supermarket, selects his food for the week, and then comes to the cash register to pay, the grocer will look to his forehead. If he sees no mark there, he will say, "May I see the palm of your hand?" If there is no mark in the hand, then he will say, "I am sorry. I cannot accept your money. If the Emperor should find out, it would mean my death and the death of my wife and children."

Think of the horror! The hunger and pain! What a terrible period of time it will be! How many people do you think will refuse the mark of the Beast when they become weak with hunger and are gnawing with pain? Yet, when one receives the mark of the Beast, he is damned.

Also, during the Tribulation period, a noisome and grievous sore shall attack those who have accepted the mark of the Beast.

Conclusion

God has extended unto all of us this day of grace. While the grace of God flows free like a river, why not repent of sin and believe upon Him? The time is coming when His mercy shall be turned into wrath, His love and longsuffering into judgment.

Although, in the day of Antichrist the world will be glorying in the Man of Sin, the great Emperor, they will be ignorant of the Word of God which says, "Behold, the day of the Lord cometh . . . For I will gather all nations against Jerusalem to battle" (Zechariah 14:1, 2). That will be the great battle called Armageddon.

The Antichrist will have become so exalted he will lead the kings of the earth and their armies out to make war against the King of Kings and Lord of Lords.

That is when the King of Kings and Lord of Lords shall step from His place in glory, mount a beautiful white stallion, and with crowns of gold upon His head go forth to fight against the Antichrist. The Lord shall destroy the Antichrist, and the armies of the world will perish. Their dead bodies shall be a great feast for the fowls of the air.

The Bible says the Antichrist shall be destroyed with the brightness of His coming. The second coming of Jesus Christ will mean the destruction of the forces of this earth. The kingdoms of this world shall become the kingdoms of the Lord our Savior; and He shall reign for ever and ever.

God speed the day when peace and righteousness shall reign upon the earth, when Jesus Christ shall sit supreme as King of the world.

Where will you be on that day?

Let us pray.

I pray, Father, Your grace and mercy upon all who read this message. Instill within us a reverence for Your Word. Lead us to take seriously the warnings You give and to find hope in the promises You make. Our hope lies in the redemption promised and accomplished by Jesus Christ upon the cross of Calvary. By faith

*in Him we rest our case and our eternal future.
In His name we pray. Amen.*

For then shall be great tribulation, such as
was not since the beginning of the world
to this time, no, nor ever shall be. And except
those days should be shortened, there should
no flesh be saved: but for the elect's sake those
days shall be shortened. Then if any man
shall say unto you, Lo, here is Christ,
or there; believe it not. For there shall arise
false Christs, and false prophets, and shall
shew great signs and wonders; insomuch that,
if it were possible, they shall deceive the very
elect. Behold, I have told you before. Wherefore
if they shall say unto you, Behold, he is
in the desert; go not forth: behold, he is in the
secret chambers; believe it not. For as the
lightning cometh out of the east, and shineth
even unto the west; so shall also the coming
of the Son of man be. . . . Immediately after
the tribulation of those days shall the sun be
darkened, and the moon shall not give her
light, and the stars shall fall from heaven, and
the powers of the heavens shall be shaken:
And then shall appear the sign of the Son of
man in heaven: and then shall all the tribes
of the earth mourn, and they shall see
the Son of man coming in the clouds of
heaven with power and great glory
(Matthew 24:21-30).

The Tribulation Period

4

Introduction

The Rapture of the church is not the end of the world. However, it is the opinion of many people that the coming of the Lord Jesus Christ will bring the end of the world.

The Word of God gives us a very detailed outline of the events that will take place upon the earth after the church has been raptured. There will be multiplied thousands of unbelievers left upon the earth to go through the most horrible, terrifying period known to humankind, a time Biblical scholars understand to be the Tribulation.

While Christians have suffered tribulation and persecution during all ages, and even though it may be correct for any of us at times to pass through a period of tribulation, we are not to confuse such normal periods of Satanic oppression or spiritual warfare with that time of *Tribulation* to which the Bible refers.

The Day of Jacob's Trouble

In speaking of this specific Tribulation period, Jesus

THE RAPTURE AND REVELATION

said, "For then shall be great tribulation, such as was not since the beginning of the world to this time, no, nor ever shall be" (Matthew 24:21).

Jeremiah prophesied of those days of anguish in these words:

> Ask ye now, and see whether a man doth travail with child? wherefore do I see every man with his hands on his loins, as a woman in travail, and all faces are turned into paleness? Alas! for that day is great, so that none is like it: it is even the time of Jacob's trouble; but he shall be saved out of it (Jeremiah 30:6, 7).

Isaiah called it a day of indignation.

> Come, my people, enter thou into thy chambers, and shut thy doors about thee: hide thyself as it were for a little moment, until the indignation be overpast. For, behold, the Lord cometh out of his place to punish the inhabitants of the earth for their iniquity: the earth also shall disclose her blood, and shall no more cover her slain (Isaiah 26:20, 21).

All the unbelievers who are left on earth when the church has been caught away will have to face this horrible time of God's judgments. Some morning, evening, or midnight hour, without warning or announcement, those who are in Christ will suddenly disappear from their homes, schools, offices and businesses. People from all walks of life and all ages will suddenly be gone.

The wife will possibly inquire, "What makes my husband late coming home tonight?"

Conversations will be interrupted. One person will vanish and the other will be left in consternation. In many cases, a portion of the family will be gone and the others left. The same anxious question will occupy the whole of humanity. In the home, on the streets, in the factories or wherever people are, they will be asking, "Where have they gone?"

The crowds of the earth will go into hysteria when they hear the radio and television announcements, when they read the newspaper extras announcing that people are missing en masse. Without warning or announcement thousands have vanished in the greatest mass disappearance story of all history.

Cries, shrieks and wails will rend the air. Schools will be closed. Night clubs will have no customers. Stadiums will be empty. Joyful music will be turned into mourning. Men's appetites will leave them. Business will be paralyzed and the wheels of industry will come to a screeching halt. Many government agency posts will be left vacant, and the whole world's economic and business infrastructure will go into severe shock. When through mass communications it is realized this dreadful visitation fell at the same moment upon the entire world, the shock will be all the more pervasive.

But all of this will be just the beginning of sorrows.

After the Rapture

The Tribulation period will follow the Rapture of the church. By Tribulation period, we mean a seven-year space of time between the two events of the coming of Christ. Now, if you do not get it clear in your mind that the coming of Christ is one advent with two phases, you can never fully understand the Tribulation period.

First, Jesus Christ comes in mid air and catches away the dead and the living saints together with Him in the clouds. We can refer to this as phase one of the second coming of Christ.

When the Tribulation period is finished, Christ will appear with His saints to establish His kingdom upon the earth. This is phase two of the second coming of Christ.

The period between the rapture of the saints and His coming back with the saints is called the Tribulation period. This period will last for approximately seven years. The final three and one-half years is called the Great Tribulation. The first few weeks and months after the saints of God are gone, men will have the job of reconstructing a shattered society. Vacant offices will have to be filled. In some quarters, new store clerks will be hired, new managers for businesses and presidents for firms will have to be decided upon. Some government posts will have to be filled, and there will need to be a complete reorganization of the affairs of the world.

There will be thousands who cannot believe their eyes and will be panic-stricken. They will continue for months in search of relatives and companions that are gone, only to come to the realization that the message of the coming of the Lord Jesus Christ was a reality—the church has been translated and they have been left upon this earth to face the judgments of Almighty God.

> While the whole world is in a state of shock, the devil will take advantage of this opportunity. The Bible tells, And then shall that Wicked be revealed,

whom the Lord shall consume with the spirit of his mouth, and shall destroy with the brightness of his coming: Even him, whose coming is after the working of Satan with all power and signs and lying wonders, And with all deceivableness of unrighteousness in them that perish; because they received not the love of the truth, that they might be saved. And for this cause God shall send them strong delusion, that they should believe a lie: That they all might be damned who believed not the truth, but had pleasure in unrighteousness (2 Thessalonians 2:8-12).

Rise of Antichrist

At the beginning of this Tribulation period, the Antichrist shall be revealed (v. 8), and those who would not believe the truth of the Lord Jesus Christ will believe the lies of the Antichrist. For even Jesus said, "I am come in my Father's name, and ye receive me not: if another shall come in his own name, him ye will receive" (John 5:43).

During this confused and frustrated state, the lost of the world will grasp for a straw of hope. The Antichrist will gain prominence as a world leader through the power of Satan.

The Bible says, "Even him, whose coming is after the working of Satan with all power and signs and lying wonders" (2 Thessalonians 2:9). He will rise to prominence and receive universal acclaim as the leader of the world. He will become the imperial head of the reorganized Roman Empire, which is already well on its way toward reorganization.

This new world leader known as the Antichrist—called the Beast in the book of Revelation (Revelation 13)—will sway the world with his power. Men will rejoice in him, not realizing that it is Satan who has given this beast his power and authority.

A Covenant with the Jews

The Antichrist will begin his reign under the guise of peace and prosperity. One of his first acts will be to make a covenant with the Jews for the seven-year period. According to the prophet Daniel, "He shall confirm the covenant with many for one week" (Daniel 9:27). That is a week of years—seven years. But the Bible goes on to say in that same verse, "And in the midst of the week he shall cause the sacrifice and the oblation to cease, and for the overspreading of abominations he shall make it desolate."

This simply means the Antichrist will deceive the Jews for the first three-and-one-half years, but then the covenant shall be broken. When the beast sets himself up as God and demands the worship of the Jews, they will realize they have been deceived.

The Antichrist will rebuild the Temple at Jerusalem and claim to be God. The Scripture tells us, "Who opposeth and exalteth himself above all that is called God, or that is worshipped; so that he as God sitteth in the temple of God, shewing himself that he is God" (2 Thessalonians 2:4).

A metallic image of himself will be set up in the temple and he will call upon the Jews to worship it. The Antichrist will take the place of Jesus Christ, and deny God and His only begotten Son. The Antichrist assumes deity. This is what Jesus Christ called the abomination of desolation. "When ye therefore shall see the abomination of desolation, spoken of by Daniel the prophet, stand in the holy place, (whoso readeth, let him understand)" (Matthew 24:15).

False Prophet

Another beast, called the False Prophet, will also appear on the scene. He will exercise all the power of the Antichrist before him. The False Prophet will be the proponent of this new religion instituted by the Antichrist. Through magical, Satanical power, the False Prophet shall cause the image of the Antichrist to breathe, to speak and to appear to be alive. He shall cause "the earth and them that dwell therein to worship the first beast, whose deadly wound was healed" (Revelation 13:12).

In order that every living soul shall bow and submit to the new decrees of the False Prophet, everyone will be ordered to make an allegiance to the Antichrist by displaying a mark in his right hand or in his forehead. The Bible says, "And that no man might buy or sell, save he that had the mark, or the name of the beast, or the number of his name" (Revelation 13:17). The failure of the Jews to bow down and worship the Antichrist will result in another great extermination.

The Great Tribulation

The covenant of peace which the Antichrist will establish with the Jews will not last (Daniel 9:27 and Revelation 6:4). Multitudes will be beheaded for the Word of God and the testimony of Jesus Christ. The Antichrist is depicted as riding a red horse, symbolic of the blood of war. The Scripture says that he shall "take peace from the earth" (Revelation 6:4). The Tribulation period shall be a time of wars such as the world has never known. It is true that today there are many wars throughout the world. But during the Tribulation period every semblance of peace will be removed from the earth and the whole world will be thrown into consternation.

Now, the church is in the world, preserving it from total corruption. The church is the restraining force to hold back the floodgates of evil. But then the church will be gone. Its light will no longer shine. Its influence will no longer be felt. The full impact of evil will break loose upon the earth.

Can you imagine what this world would be without a church, without a true minister, without a radio broadcast where the gospel is preached, without a television program calling people to God and without pulpits sounding forth the truth of God? What kind of a world would that be?

Severe Famine

Not only will war riddle this period, but it will also be a time of severe famine.

> And when he had opened the third seal, I heard the third beast say, Come and see. And I beheld, and lo a black horse; and he that sat on him had a pair of balances in his hand. And I heard a voice in the midst of the four beasts say, A measure of wheat for a penny, and three measures of barley for a penny (Revelation 6:5, 6).

In this day of the Great Tribulation, there will be chronic scarcity of food, making it probable that individuals will accept the mark of the Beast in the palms of their hands or in their foreheads in order to buy food to satisfy their starving bodies. Not only will the people be affected, but the whole of creation will feel the impact of the judgment of God.

Earthquakes

The Bible says,

> And I beheld when he had opened the sixth seal, and, lo, there was a great earthquake; and the sun became black as sackcloth of hair, and the moon became as blood; And the stars of heaven fell unto the earth, even as a fig tree casteth her untimely figs, when she is shaken of a mighty wind. And the heaven departed as a scroll when it is rolled together; and every mountain and island were moved out of their places (Revelation 6:12-14).

The sun will pull a veil over its face, and the moon will begin to bleed. The stars will fall from their sockets, the heavens will roll up like a scroll and the mountains will tremble and move out of their places. God's creation will express its wrath against humanity who has rejected the Lord and Savior Jesus Christ and has trampled under foot the blood of the Son of God.

When the earth begins to rock to and fro like a drunkard and moves out of its place like a cottage in a hurricane, the greatest prayer meeting the world has ever known will take place.

It will not be a prayer meeting where people will pray for salvation from sins. They will pray for deliverance from their gnawing, guilty consciences and for a place to hide from the wrath of God.

The Bible says,

> And the kings of the earth, and the great men, and the rich men, and the chief captains, and the mighty men, and every bondman, and every free man, hid themselves in the dens and in the rocks of the mountains; And said to the mountains and rocks, Fall on us, and hide us from the face of him that sitteth on the throne, and from the wrath of the Lamb: For the great day of his wrath is come; and who shall be able to stand? (Revelation 6:15-17).

People will seek to hide from the face of Him whom they have rejected. The Bible says they shall look upon Him whom they have pierced (v. 1:7). Horrors too numerous to mention will be manifested during this Tribulation period.

As this Tribulation period nears its consummation, the Antichrist will have things well in hand; but, in his conceit, he will gather an army together to fight against God. This battle, the Battle of Armageddon, will be his downfall. The Lord shall come from heaven in the brightness of His glory and shall destroy the Antichrist and establish His kingdom upon this earth.

Conclusion

The news media reminds us constantly of trouble spots in our world. Earthquakes, tornadoes, hurricanes, storms, drought, famine—these are common occurrences that let us know pain, sorrow, death and destruction remain the common lot of man upon this earth. We sympathize with those who suffer, even when knowing we have been spared. Nevertheless, that which is happening now is but a token of what will come on this earth during the time of the Great Tribulation.

Only Jesus Christ offers a means of escape. In Him, the only begotten Son of God, there is a place of refuge. Through Him, the returning triumphant Lord, there is sure and certain promise of escape. And so I ask, are you confident of your relationship to Christ Jesus? Is He your sure and certain hope, now and forever? He can be.

If you want to escape the judgments of the Tribulation that are coming upon the earth, it is time now for you to give yourself to God. Today is the day of salvation. Now is the accepted time. "Seek ye the Lord while he may be found, call ye upon him while he is near" (Isaiah 55:6). Today is the only time that you can claim for your own. Tomorrow belongs to God. "Boast not thyself of to morrow; for thou knowest not what a day may bring forth" (Proverbs 27:1).

Let us pray.

> *Father in heaven, we honor You this moment as judge of all the earth. We trust Your love as expressed through Jesus Christ. We believe Your promise of redemption, by grace, through faith alone. And we believe Your promise of deliverance from that time of Great Tribulation that is to come upon this earth and upon those who reject you. May Your reassuring presence be with us always and may our lives reflect the moral values and beauty of Christ our Lord. In the name of Jesus we pray. Amen.*

And his feet shall stand in that day upon the mount of Olives, which is before Jerusalem on the east, and the mount of Olives shall cleave in the midst thereof toward the east and toward the west, and there shall be a very great valley; and half of the mountain shall remove toward the north, and half of it toward the south. And ye shall flee to the valley of the mountains; for the valley of the mountains shall reach unto Azal: yea, ye shall flee, like as ye fled from before the earthquake in the days of Uzziah king of Judah: and the Lord my God shall come, and all the saints with thee (Zechariah 14:4, 5).

5

How Near Is the Coming of Christ?

Introduction

How near is the coming of the Lord? This is a question asked by honest-hearted Christians the world over. In order for us to understand this question, we must first understand what is meant by the second coming of Christ. The Bible declares that He will come again the second time: "Unto them that look for him shall he appear the second time without sin unto salvation" (Hebrews 9:28).

Understanding His Coming

There are three Greek words used in the New Testament to depict the coming of Christ.

The first word, *parousia,* describes the coming of Jesus Christ as a personal bodily appearance. If Jesus Christ left the world with a body—and we know He did (Acts 1:1-9)—we also know He is coming again in bodily appearance. For the Bible is explicit: "This same Jesus, which is taken up from you into heaven, shall so come in like manner as ye have seen him go into heaven" (v. 11).

The second Greek word is *epiphaneia,* which means "His appearing." Several times in Scripture, the coming of the Lord is referred to as the appearing.

- "When Christ, who is our life, shall appear, then shall ye also appear with him in glory" (Colossians 3:4).

- "Beloved, now are we the sons of God, and it doth not yet appear what we shall be: but we know that, when he shall appear, we shall be like him; for we shall see him as he is" (1 John 3:2).

- "When the chief Shepherd shall appear, ye shall receive a crown of glory that fadeth not away" (1 Peter 5:4).

- "I charge thee therefore before God, and the Lord Jesus Christ, who shall judge the quick and the dead at his appearing and his kingdom" (2 Timothy 4:1).

- "Looking for that blessed hope, and the glorious appearing of the great God and our Saviour Jesus Christ" (Titus 2:13).

The third Greek word used for the coming of the Lord is *apokalupsis,* which means "the unveiling or revelation."

The first two words are used in connection with the Rapture, or the catching away of the saints to meet the Lord in the air; but *apokalupsis,* means the person of Christ will be revealed at the Second Coming to earth. The Bible says, "Behold, he cometh with clouds; and every eye shall see him, and they also which pierced him: and all kindreds of the earth shall wail because of him" (Revelation 1:7).

We must then understand that the coming again of the Lord Jesus Christ is one advent with two different stages. First, He comes in mid-air when all who are in Christ shall be caught up to meet Him in the air. Secondly, He shall come with His saints to establish His kingdom on earth.

One reason so many people are confused about the coming of the Lord is that they do not understand the two different stages or phases of His coming. While the saints of God are caught up with Christ, a period called the Tribulation, or the Seventieth Week of Daniel, will take place upon the earth. At the end of this period of judgment, Christ shall come with His saints to overcome the Antichrist, to fight the Battle of Armageddon and to establish His millennial kingdom on this earth.

The Bible says,

> And his feet shall stand in that day upon the mount of Olives, which is before Jerusalem on the east, and the mount of Olives shall cleave in the midst thereof toward the east and toward the west, and there shall be a very great valley; and half of the mountain shall remove toward the north, and half of it toward the south. And ye shall flee to the valley of the mountains; for the valley of the mountains shall reach unto Azal: yea, ye shall flee, like as ye fled from before the earthquake in the days of Uzziah king of Judah: and the Lord my God shall come, and all the saints with thee (Zechariah 14:4, 5).

Date Setting

There are those who will attempt to set the exact date of Christ's return. But it is in God's plan that we should be kept in uncertainty on this point. Setting dates and declaring that Christ will come at a certain hour is out of harmony with the Scriptures. Jesus Christ said,

- "Watch therefore; for ye know not what hour your Lord doth come" (Matthew 24:42).

- "Therefore be ye also ready: for in such an hour as ye think not the Son of man cometh" (v. 44).

- "Take ye heed, watch and pray: for ye know not when the time is" (Mark 13:33).

- "Watch ye therefore: for ye know not when the master of the house cometh, at even, or at midnight, or at the cockcrowing, or in the morning: Lest coming suddenly he find you sleeping" (v. 35, 36).

Since it is impossible for us to know the exact date of His coming, we must leave that matter to the Lord. The most common fallacy in our time is that some eager-hearted people attempt to set dates and thus confuse the minds of the people concerning the coming of the Lord. That is what happened in the Thessalonian church. Paul wrote his letter to them, instructing them that certain things had to happen before the day of Christ could come. To confuse the minds of the people concerning the coming of the Lord is one of the greatest tools of the devil. We do not know the exact date nor hour, but that does not mean that we cannot know when the coming of the Lord draws near.

Unbelief of His Coming

Almost all of the world and the majority of church members do not actually believe that Jesus Christ could come today. In fact, many people have heard the message of the coming of Christ preached over and over until they have assumed the attitude that it is merely a much-repeated warning and could not happen in their generation. As a result, the church sleeps on, at ease in Zion, lukewarm, and indifferent, saying, "My Lord delayeth His coming."

The apostle Peter warns us, "Knowing this first, that there shall come in the last days scoffers, walking after their own lusts, And saying, Where is the promise of his coming?" (2 Peter 3:3, 4).

Peter implies that it is not because they have not been warned, or could not know, or that they had not heard, for he said, "For this they willingly are ignorant of" (3:5).

Their attitude is like those in the days of Jeremiah. They defy the Lord by asking the question, "Where is the Word of the Lord? let it come now" (Jeremiah 17:15).

They are like those in the days of Isaiah, who said, "Let him make speed, and hasten his work, that we may see it: and let the counsel of the Holy One of Israel draw nigh and come, that we may know it!" (Isaiah 5:19).

Like those in the days of Ezekiel, they mock, saying, "The vision that he seeth is for many days to come, and he prophesieth of the times that are far off" (Ezekiel 12:27).

The prophet Amos, too, had a word to say on this attitude, "Ye that put far away the evil day, and cause the seat of violence to come near" (Amos 6:3).

The attitude of this time, both in the world and in the church, is the thing that stirs my heart. I realize that few people actually know that Jesus Christ could come today, for He declares in His Word that it will be just such a time as this when He comes: "For the Son of man cometh at an hour when ye think not" (Luke 12:40).

If I were to ask, "Do you think the Lord could come in the next 24 hours?" you would possibly say, "I think not." If we did believe Jesus could come at any moment, this glorious event would occupy our thinking, and we would make all of our decisions with this thought in mind. It would provoke and inspire us to consistent Christian living every day.

Because many feel that the coming of the Lord has been delayed, they have become earthbound and attached to this present world and its values. They live as though they will live forever on this earth. Spiritual sight is clouded. Spiritual sensitivity is callused. Love has grown cold. Spiritual fire is waning. Their attitude toward evangelism is passive. The church has become a mere convenience and they are absorbed in this present world. As a general rule, they no longer anticipate the coming of the Lord as in years gone by.

Because of this attitude, I am constrained to echo the words of the apostle Paul "And that, knowing the time, that now it is high time to awake out of sleep: for now is our salvation nearer than when we believed" (Romans 13:11).

Imminence of His Coming

Though some Bible scholars object to the thought, I believe there is not a single Bible event that must yet come to pass before the Savior returns. I believe all prophetic utterances that must take place have in truth already taken place and that Jesus Christ could appear in the clouds of glory at any moment.

Those who argue otherwise will quote, "This gospel of the kingdom shall be preached in all the world for a witness unto all nations; and then shall the end come" (Matthew 24:14). They then conclude that this has not happened; and, since it has not happened, Christ cannot yet come.

But the coming of the Lord Jesus Christ for His saints is not the end of the world: it is merely the end of the church age, when the saints shall be taken out of the world. When Jesus talks about the imminence of His coming, He always refers to the first stage of His coming, the Rapture, when the church is caught away from the world.

The end of the world will not take place until the time comes when the Kingdom shall be delivered up to the Father—"Then cometh the end" (1 Corinthians 15:24). This is the end of the thousand-year reign of Christ on earth.

The Lord could come at any moment and all of us who believe must be watching and waiting for His appearing.

Signs of His Coming

Again, there are those who have confused the two stages of the coming of the Lord. They are looking for some things to happen before the Rapture that I believe will not happen until after the church is gone. Therefore, they are complacent and at ease in their sins because these events have not taken place.

For example, some people are looking for the moon to turn into blood, for the sun to be darkened and for the stars to fall from heaven before Christ comes for His church.

The Bible says,

> Immediately after the tribulation of those days shall the sun be darkened, and the moon shall not give her light, and the stars shall fall from heaven, and the powers of the heavens shall be shaken: And then shall appear the sign of the Son of man in heaven: and then shall all the tribes of the earth mourn, and they shall see the Son of man coming in the clouds of heaven with power and great glory (Matthew 24:29, 30).

But notice, these signs are to precede the unveiling of Christ or the revelation of Christ when He comes with His saints in power and great glory to tear down the kingdoms of this world. This does not refer to the time when He comes in midair to catch away His church out of this world; or, in other words, to the Rapture.

Others say the Lord cannot come just yet because the Antichrist has not been revealed. They misinterpret the Scripture which reads,

> Now we beseech you, brethren, by the coming of our Lord Jesus Christ, and by our gathering together unto him, That ye be not soon shaken in mind, or be troubled, neither by spirit, nor by word, nor

by letter as from us, as that the day of Christ is at hand. Let no man deceive you by any means: for that day shall not come, except there come a falling away first, and that man of sin be revealed, the son of perdition (2 Thessalonians 2:1-3).

This Scripture plainly tells us that the day of Christ is not at hand and will not be until the Antichrist is revealed; but, the day of Christ must not be confused with the rapturing away of the saints.

In the ministry of Christ, He was constantly illustrating the imminence of His coming again.

He said it would be like the flood in the days of Noah when the people were eating, drinking, marrying and giving in marriage until the day that Noah entered into the ark and he knew not until the flood came and took them all away.

He said it would be like five foolish virgins who had no oil in their lamps, and when the midnight cry was given—"Behold, the bridegroom cometh; go ye out to meet him" (Matthew 25:6)—they were not prepared.

He said it would be like the man who failed to watch and the thief broke into his house unexpectedly. A thief may come at any time, without a warning, without a set time.

Therefore, it is so essential that the Christian stand on guard lest he be found bereft of those things that he holds so dear. Jesus said to take heed to yourself. Watch, therefore, pray always, for that day could come upon you suddenly, unaware, or as a snare (Luke 21:34).

In the last chapter of the last book of the Bible, the

Holy Spirit moved upon John to write three different times, "I come quickly" (Revelation: 22:7, 12, 20).

The Scriptures seem to be saying quickly, **quickly**, QUICKLY. This is what Jesus is trying to impress upon us today. I believe these three Scriptures are given to us so close together in order to impress upon us the urgency of preparing for His soon return.

Today is the day of salvation. Now is the accepted time. It could be that you would not see the light of another day. Something is about to happen. Christians and sinners, statesmen and men the world over feel that something is about to take place. Men of the world are afraid. They are trembling. They are looking for something to happen. They fear an unknown and unforeseen tragedy.

Men's hearts are failing them for fear, as they look upon those things which are coming upon the earth (Luke 21:26).

Conclusion

But if we have Christ, we need not fear. Our fears can be settled in Him who loved us and gave Himself for us.

Even now, this moment, if you would like to find peace in your heart, you may do so. Christ stands ready to forgive your sins, to give you peace, to grant you joy, and to assure you of His eternal love.

Would you bow your head in prayer?

Dear God in heaven, with humility and a realization that I am but mortal flesh, born in sin and shapen in iniquity, I seek Your mercy and forgiveness. I yearn for peace in my heart. I reach out to You, seeking redemption. I need reassurance and courage and strength, all of which can come only from You. Let it be so now, I pray in the name of Your son, Jesus Christ of Nazareth. Amen.

Now learn a parable of the fig tree;
When his branch is yet tender, and putteth
forth leaves, ye know that summer is nigh:
So likewise ye, when ye shall see all these
things, know that it is near, even at the
doors. Verily I say unto you, This generation
shall not pass, till all these things be fulfilled
(Matthew 24:32-34).

And he spake to them a parable; "Behold the fig
tree, and all the trees; When they now shoot
forth, ye see and know of your own selves that
summer is now nigh at hand. So likewise ye,
when ye see these things come to pass, know
ye that the kingdom of God is nigh at hand.
Verily I say unto you, This generation shall
not pass away, till all be fulfilled"
(Luke 21:29-32).

6

WILL THIS GENERATION SEE THE COMING OF CHRIST?

Introduction

Although these two passages of Scripture have been much debated and are highly controversial in interpretation, both are vital in these last days.

Matthew tells us, "learn a parable of the fig tree." In Scriptures the fig tree is symbolic of Israel. The Lord calls Israel "my fig tree" (Joel 1:7). Israel is God's special treasure or chosen nation through which He speaks to all mankind.

While Matthew says "Learn a parable of the fig tree," Luke says "Behold the fig tree, and all the trees."

This is not a contradiction. Matthew is writing primarily to the Jews, while the Gospel of Luke is directed to the Gentiles. The same statement, with *all the trees* added is Luke's way of including the Gentile nations.

The Parable of the Fig Tree

In this parable, Christ called our attention to a tree which in the springtime begins to reproduce by putting forth buds. The same tree that has lain dormant and dead through the cold winter months now begins to bud and flower.

The budding and flowering of trees indicates summer is near. This is a truth men have known from time immemorial.

So, Jesus uses this very simple illustration to focus our attention on a larger and major prophetic truth: when we see the once-dead nation of Israel—a people without a country and without a king—return to their own land, then shall we know the coming of the Lord is near.

In AD 70, when the Roman General Titus destroyed the Jewish temple and laid waste the city of Jerusalem, the nation of Israel ceased to exist for all practical purposes.

In fact, for a period of 1,878 years—until the present state of Israel was proclaimed on May 14, 1948—Israel can best be considered as a valley of dead, dry bones (Ezekiel 37).

Along with Ezekiel's well-known prophecy, Hosea wrote,

> For the children of Israel shall abide many days without a king, and without a prince, and without a sacrifice, and without an image, and without an ephod, and without teraphim: Afterward shall the children of Israel return, and seek the Lord their God, and David their king; and shall fear the Lord and his goodness in the latter days (Hosea 3:4, 5).

Notice this phrase *in the latter days*. For many centuries the land of Israel had been barren. Because the
judgment of God was upon the nation of Israel, the early
and latter rain had been withheld. The land had become
a howling wilderness.

About a half-century ago, things began to change in the
land of Palestine. The rainfall began to increase, and the
water level began to rise.

Lands that had lain barren for many years began to blossom again like a rose. Plantations of renown, spoken of by
Ezekiel, took the place of the desert.

The pools of Solomon, at one time empty, are now
filled with millions of gallons of water. I have seen these
beautiful pools and these other changes with my own eyes,
and I realize all these are the fulfillment of the prophecy of
God's Word.

Such is the reason for all the feverish activity now taking place in the Middle East and for the worldwide attention now focused on that part of the world. We can sel-
dom pick up a newspaper or magazine, or listen to the
evening news on radio or TV without there being some
focus on Israel and the Middle East.

The fulfillment of prophesy during these last fifty years
is an indication of how swiftly we are moving to the hour
of Christ's soon return.

The Jewish people, once without a king, without a
prince, without a government, without a flag or even a
place to call home, have risen to a nation of prominence.

Now, most all the leading powers of the world recognize
this "promised land" belongs to Israel. Blue and white
flags, with colors symbolic of garments worn by the high

priest when he entered into the holy temple on the Day of Atonement, now flutter in the wind over Jerusalem. The six-pointed star, the same star which decorated the shield of David, now waves over the little nation of Israel.

An unbelievable miracle has taken place. For hundreds of years, the Jews daily chanted these words: "Sound the great trumpet for our freedom; raise the banner for gathering our exiles; gather us together from the four corners of the earth into our own land." They no longer have to pray this prayer. Today, the fig tree is in full bloom. Israel is a nation. On that memorable day in May, 1948, a nation was literally born in a day, fulfilling Isaiah's prophecy: "Shall the earth be made to bring forth in one day? or shall a nation be born at once?" (Isaiah 66:8).

The Meaning of "All the Trees"

Luke's expression *all the trees* means the nations of the world. Is there not something to learn from all of civilization?

The feverish, devilish activity of this age, the cry for peace, the constant perplexities, the international pestilences, the many earthquakes—do these not tell us that disaster knocks at our door and that something momentous is about to happen? Jesus is saying in this parable, when the trees begin to bud and the leaves appear, spring is at hand; which, being interpreted, means we can know summer is near. We can know the coming of the Lord is at hand.

Bible scholars and social commentators all agree that these are momentous days. The average man or woman on the street seems to feel something unusual is in the air. Old nations are changing, new nations are springing forth. Some nations are referred to constantly as hot spots, nations on which the whole world focuses attention. All too often the attention traces back to the nation of Israel.

In it all, those with spiritual discernment hear an echo of the Lord's words as recorded in Matthew and Luke.

The Meaning of "This Generation"

There is something even more revealing in this passage of Scripture which I believe is hidden from the view of most Christians today. We see it in the words, "This generation shall not pass, till all these things be fulfilled" (both Matthew and Luke). This is the portion of Scripture that has been highly controversial and debatable. But I see no reason for debate at this point. The Scripture is plain and clear.

What is meant by *this generation*?

Down through the years, Bible scholars have presented three theories. Let us examine each of them briefly.

First, *this generation* means the generation living on the earth at the time Jesus was speaking. Such an interpretation is not logical, since many generations have passed and Jesus has not come.

Those who maintain this argument must also follow up with an argument that Jesus has come already and we didn't know it, a position which does not at all line up with either Scripture or known historical facts.

Second, there is a school of thought which claims the word *generation* means the nation or the race of Israel.

This is quite unlikely, because the disciples were asking for a sign of the coming of the Lord Jesus Christ. Jesus reminded them that when the fig tree begins to bud, it is a sign that summer is near.

If the word *generation* merely means *race*, the Scripture would read like this: "This race shall not pass away until all these things be accomplished." If we read it like that, then there is really no significance to the Scripture because God had already promised the "seed of Abraham" would not pass away. Such would be no special sign at all concerning the return of the Lord Jesus Christ.

Third, and what I consider the correct interpretation of this passage, *this generation* refers to those living on earth at the time these conditions mentioned in this Scripture are fulfilled.

Truth of the matter is, the word generation comes from the Greek word *genia*, which, according to Greek scholars, cannot be translated race but must be translated generation. Therefore, what Jesus was saying to the disciples is that the generation living when these signs are fulfilled is the generation that will see the coming of the Lord Jesus Christ.

When the Lord's own disciples asked the question, "What is the sign of Thy coming and the end of the world?" Jesus proceeded to relate to them some of the things that would happen on the eve of His return.

I believe it is possible for true Christians to understand the signs of the time when the coming of our Lord draws near. We need not be in the dark and in doubt about this.

The writer of Hebrews tells us, "Not forsaking the assembling of ourselves together, as the manner of some is; but exhorting one another: and so much the more, as ye see the day approaching" (Hebrews 10:25). This particular Scripture certainly implies we will be able to see the day approaching.

We have seen the budding of the fig tree. With the eyes of the world focused upon Israel, we can know that we live in one of the most momentous days of human history.

I would not attempt to say precisely just how long a period *this generation* covers. It fills my heart with soberness, however, when I realize that in my day, in my generation, I could behold the glory of the coming of the Lord.

We who are prepared for the coming of the Lord have reason to rejoice. For Jesus said, "And when these things begin to come to pass, then look up, and lift up your heads; for your redemption draweth nigh" (Luke 21:28). Already we have gone far past the beginning of these things. We have good reason to lift up our eyes to the skies and prepare our hearts for the journey to the shores of sweet deliverance.

The Context of This Scripture

Let us examine the context of Matthew 24:32-34. Two verses later we read, "But of that day and hour knoweth no man, no, not the angels of Heaven, but my Father only" (v. 36). Jesus Christ is following His statement, "This generation shall not pass away till all these things be fulfilled" with these words, "No man, not even the angels of Heaven, but the Father only, knows the day and the hour of the coming of the Son of Man." In other words, no one knows the exact date, the exact time or the exact hour when the Lord will return.

But Jesus' words do strengthen my interpretation of this statement when He says, "But as the days of Noe were, so shall also the coming of the Son of man be. For as in the days that were before the flood they were eating and drinking, marrying and giving in marriage, until the day that Noe entered into the ark" (vv. 37, 38).

In other words, as in the days of Noah that were before the flood, they were eating, drinking, marrying, and giving in marriage until the day that Noah entered into the ark. They knew not until the flood came and took them all away.

So shall the coming of the Son of Man be. Although we do not know the exact day or hour of the coming of the Son of Man, we do know the conditions that will exist in the day of His coming. Therefore, we have full right to believe that, when we see these things happening around us, the coming of the Lord is near. God's Word is true. The promise of Jesus that, "I will come again," is about to be fulfilled.

Conclusion

If this generation is the closing generation of this age, then this is the day for which all Christians have looked and for which all have longed.

I believe this generation *will* see the coming of the Lord.

Are you prepared to meet Jesus? Are you living for the world to come, or are you burdened down with this present world?

Let me warn you in the words of the apostle Peter, "Wherefore, beloved, seeing that ye look for such things, be diligent that ye may be found of him in peace, without spot, and blameless" (2 Peter 3:14).

Let us pray.

> *Forgive us our sins, Oh God, that our hearts be tuned to heavenly things. Create within us obedient hearts. Give us eyes to see and ears to hear what You are saying to your people. Sanctify us through Your precious blood and let us be ever hopeful and ever ready for Your coming again, in power and in glory. Amen.*

*And as it was in the days of Noe, so
shall it be also in the days of the Son
of man. They did eat, they drank, they
married wives, they were given in marriage,
until the day that Noe entered into the ark,
and the flood came, and destroyed them
all. Likewise also as it was in the days
of Lot; they did eat, they drank, they bought,
they sold, they planted, they builded;
But the same day that Lot went out of
Sodom it rained fire and brimstone from
heaven, and destroyed them all. Even thus
shall it be in the day when the
Son of man is revealed*
(Luke 17:26-30).

7

As in the Days of Noah and Lot

Introduction

It is very revealing that Jesus Christ compared life on earth during the last days with life on earth during the days of Noah and during the time of Abraham and Lot. This was more than a casual reference. Jesus was very specific in His description, mentioning family life and sexual attitudes, social and economic conditions, as well as spiritual and moral values.

Our Lord's words were spoken in answer to direct questions posed by the disciples on the Mount of Olives. They asked, "What shall be the sign of thy coming, and of the end of the world?" (Matthew 24:3).

There is little debate or question as to what Jesus meant when He answered these questions. He fully intended to give signs and to explain what things would be like when His return drew near. This sign of the times is couched within a graphic comparison between life as known during the days of Noah and Lot and life as experienced by the generation that will witness the return of Christ. Similar lifestyles, similar conditions, similar attitudes—these are to remind us, "Even thus shall it be in the day when the Son of man is revealed" (Luke 17:30).

Our task is to examine and fully understand what life was all about back then. Just what was happening on this earth when God decided to destroy civilization with a flood? What was going on in the city of Sodom when God chose to rain down fire and brimstone?

Rejection of God

When we read the Book of Genesis and compare it with the sins of our day, we must marvel at the detail and precision with which Christ portrays these days. Using the simple phrase, "As it was then . . . so shall it be," He gives a message frightening to those of this world but at the same time gloriously full of redemptive grace for the believer. The Lord's first and most obvious sign is a reminder that in the days of Noah and Lot there was rejection of God.

For several decades Noah preached righteousness to his generation but he was able to convince only seven others, those of his own household, of the righteousness of God. Men and women just would not believe God's judgment was coming. They disdained Noah's message. They thought life would continue as it was.

The apostle Peter writes of God's judgment in these words of his first epistle, "The longsuffering of God waited in the days of Noah, while the ark was a preparing, wherein few, that is, eight souls were saved by water" (1 Peter 3:20); then later, in his second epistle by saying, "God spared not . . . the old world, but saved Noah the eighth person, a preacher of righteousness, bringing in the flood upon the world of the ungodly" (2 Peter 2:4, 5).

Noah was an upright man who found favor in the eyes of God, but the men and women of his day would not heed his message.

The same was true in the days of Lot, when Abraham prayed for Lot and his safekeeping. Upon hearing that God intended to destroy the cities of Sodom and Gomorrah, Abraham interceded, praying God to spare the righteous living there (Genesis 18:20-33). He was able to persuade God to promise the withholding of judgment if a mere 10 righteous people could be found.

It was not to be. Only three people, Lot and his two daughters, were delivered from the judgment of Sodom and Gomorrah. The Bible tells us, "Then the Lord rained upon Sodom and upon Gomorrah brimstone and fire from the Lord out of heaven; And he overthrew those cities, and all the plain, and all the inhabitants of the cities, and that which grew upon the ground. . . . And Abraham gat up early in the morning to the place where he stood before the Lord: And he looked toward Sodom and Gomorrah, and toward all the land of the plain, and beheld, and, lo, the smoke of the country went up as the smoke of a furnace" (19:24-28).

This is clear evidence that the population before the flood and during the days of Lot had almost totally rejected God. God was not at all in their thoughts.

Brute Physical Lust

Another condition of the days of Noah and Lot set forth

by the Lord Jesus Christ was what the gospel writer phrased as *eating and drinking*. The meaning of this phrase, of course, denotes more than the mere act of eating food and drinking beverages. There is nothing wrong with eating and drinking in terms of hunger and thirst. These are both necessary for the existence of the human race. The *eating* as referenced here means over-indulgence, gluttony, living to satisfy sensual appetites.

The apostle Paul properly described this sort of people when speaking of the enemies of Christ, "Whose end is destruction, whose God is their belly, and whose glory is in their shame, who mind earthly things" (Philippians 3:19).

Jesus Christ warned us, "Take heed to yourselves, lest at any time your hearts be overcharged with surfeiting, and drunkenness, and cares of this life, and so that day come upon you unawares. For as a snare shall it come on all them that dwell on the face of the whole earth" (Luke 21:34, 35).

We are not to make the satisfactions of the physical man the main purpose and object of life.

When Christ refers to *drinking* there is no doubt but what he is speaking of alcoholic beverages and drunkenness. Seventy percent of the teenagers who have taken up the habit of drinking testify that they began drinking in their own homes where it was available from their own refrigerators. Seventy-four percent of all students in universities and colleges drink alcoholic beverages. More young women are employed as barmaids, in nightclubs, honky-tonks, and other houses of vice, than are attending colleges and universities.

Drinking has become so dominant that anyone who doesn't participate is almost considered a social outcast.

Social pressure is brought to bear upon people in our generation until they feel as though they are not a part of this young society unless they drink. Businessmen feel that they must take a social drink in order to maintain their jobs. Business and promotional meetings circle around "happy hour" and evening cocktails.

When you see and hear all the advertising of alcoholic beverages or read of an accident on the highway where lives were called out into eternity, when you read of men with delirium tremens who have lost their balance and ruined their family name, when you hear of divorces caused by alcoholism, children made orphans and homes broken up, then be reminded of the words of Jesus Christ. In the days just prior to the coming of the Son of man, it will be as it was in the days of Noah—eating and drinking.

Multiple Marriages and Divorce

The gospel writer's phrase is, "marrying and giving in marriage" (Matthew 24:38). The breakup of the American home has become so pronounced and so accepted that sociologists and secular youth counselors now warn the young to be prepared for at least three careers and three marriages during a normal lifetime. Even in the days of Noah and Lot marriage had become a mere convenience for the satisfaction of sensual desires. Men married for lust rather than for love. Marriage bonds were cut at the least provocation, and the sacredness and sanctity of the holy union of marriage were no longer considered in the light of God's command.

This condition becomes increasingly worse by the year, until now one out of every three couples who stand before the minister with the blush of youth in their cheeks and the spark of love in their eyes, taking their marriage vows, will soon be looking for another lover, a new partner, a new thrill. This all comes from a warped idea of marriage and a disregard for the command of God that a man should be the husband of one wife.

We are faced not only with divorces, sins of infidelity and adultery, but with the prominence of one of the most horrid, disgusting and putrid sins of all times—the sin of sodomy or homosexuality.

Jude states this sin was prominent in the days of Lot and notes the judgment of God, "Even as Sodom and Gomorrah, and the cities about them in like manner, giving themselves over to fornication, and going after strange flesh, are set forth for an example, suffering the vengeance of eternal fire" (Jude 7). The vivid details of this horrible story are recorded in Genesis, chapter 19.

The cry of wickedness, immorality and violence was so great during the days of Sodom the Bible says, "But the men of Sodom were wicked and sinners before the Lord *exceedingly*" (Genesis 13:13).

> And the Lord said, Because the cry of Sodom and Gomorrah is great, and because their sin is very grievous; I will go down now, and see whether they have done altogether according to the cry of it, which is come unto me; and if not, I will know (18:20, 21).

In chapter 19 it is revealed that God sent two angels to Sodom, and out of that large city there was only one logical place for them to lodge. There was only one righteous family, only one believing family, in the city of Sodom.

That family was Lot's, and even a portion of his family had already been tainted by the corruption of Sodom.

When the men of the town heard that visitors were being entertained by Lot, the sordid story began to unfold. Scripture says,

> But before they lay down, the men of the city, even the men of Sodom, compassed the house round, both old and young, all the people from every quarter: And they called unto Lot, and said unto him, Where are the men which came in to thee this night? bring them out unto us, that we may know them (Genesis 19:4, 5).

Here is where the sin of homosexuality received its name of sodomy, the first Biblical mention or record of this debasing sin. Sodom had so deteriorated until the Bible says that this was a common sin, not only of the old, but of the young men as well. This is the thing that happens when man begins to worship the creature instead of the Creator.

Unlike many social commentators today, those ultra-sensitive to what is politically correct, the Word of God does not take a hush-hush attitude toward the subject of homosexuality (gays and lesbians). Paul is very explicit when he writes to the church at Rome,

> For this cause God gave them up unto vile affections: for even their women did change the natural use into that which is against nature: And likewise also the men, leaving the natural use of the woman, burned in their lust one toward another; men with men working that which is unseemly,

and receiving in themselves that recompense of their error which was meet (Romans 1:26, 27).

Writing to the Corinthians Paul speaks of this sin using the term "abusers of themselves with mankind" (1 Corinthians 6:9). In his first epistle to Timothy he speaks of "whoremongers [and] them that defile themselves with mankind" (1 Timothy 1:10).

Today this sin, which is a stench in the nostrils of God and which should cause the public to bow their heads in shame, is prominent in government circles, in schools and universities, in community gangs and clubs, and in special organized societies. Men, burning in their own lusts, are seeking satisfaction for their bestial nature. Almost daily the newspapers reveal stories of sexual orgies and perversion that would infuriate and make any sane person righteously indignant. I am aware that this is a horrible picture to paint, but it is, nevertheless, very true. We must not close our eyes to the fact that the Bible says, "And as it was in the days of Noe, so shall it be also in the days of the Son of man" (Luke 17:26).

These things existed, and today they exist in even a more pronounced manner than most of us are aware.

Pornographic literature now often published under the guise of art is used to inflame passions and promote the sex crimes of our time. Pornography has become a multibillion-dollar business. This business grows on public demand for filth and these filth factories grind out sensual garbage for the consumption of youth and every age group of our generation. Unless God gives a revival, our future is bleak indeed, for we stand on the brink of damnation.

Filthy Conversation

The Word of God reveals another condition of the days of Lot. It speaks of a "just Lot, vexed with the filthy conversation of the wicked" (2 Peter 2:7). Vulgar, indecent, filthy conversation was common among the people of Lot's day.

Today, the air reeks with profanity, crude jokes and filthy conversation. One can hardly talk with the average man or woman on the street without being subjected to this verbal barrage of wickedness. Such conversation reveals the depravity of the human heart. The Bible says, "For as he thinketh in his heart, so is he" (Proverbs 23:7). Jesus said, "A good man out of the good treasure of the heart bringeth forth good things: and an evil man out of the evil treasure bringeth forth evil things" (Matthew 12:35).

Such was also the condition in the days of Noah, "And God saw that the wickedness of man was great in the earth, and that every imagination of the thoughts of his heart was only evil continually" (Genesis 6:5).

Material Prosperity

The days of Noah and Lot were also times of great material achievement. The Bible says of that day, "They bought, they sold, they planted, they builded" (Luke 17:28). Now, while these things are essential for the well-being and welfare of humanity, Christ is letting us know that materialism dominated the day.

Likewise, men have become so materialistic in our time that commercialism and the greedy search for worldly gain has drowned spirituality and all sense of propriety. Men and women today have no time for Almighty God.

The Word of God warns us about becoming so engrossed in these times and so busy with the cares of this life that the Judgment Day shall overtake us unaware, "For in such an hour that ye think not the Son of man cometh" (Matthew 24:44).

That is exactly what happened in the days of Noah and Lot. People were engrossed in the things of this life, wrapped up in sensual pleasures and appetites. They had a false sense of carnal security which caused them to give no thought to the coming judgment of God. In the face of Noah's preaching, men laughed. Even the sons-in-law of Lot mocked when he told them of God's sure and certain coming judgment.

The true gospel ministry of our day is receiving similar treatment at the hands of a world doomed but not yet aware of it. The Bible says this was the conduct of those in the days of Noah, until the day that Noah entered into the ark and the flood came and destroyed them all. It was the same conduct of those in the day of Lot until the day that Lot went out of Sodom and it rained fire and brimstone from heaven and destroyed them all. Notice this, "Even thus shall it be in the day when the Son of man is revealed" (Luke 17:30).

Conclusion

The Word of God is plainly setting forth here that the coming of the Lord will take place when least expected. He will come as a "thief in the night" (1 Thessalonians 5:2). He will come suddenly, "in a moment, in the twinkling of an eye" (1 Corinthians 15:52). Just as the antediluvians were not aware of the preaching of righteousness until Noah was safe within the ark, and "The Lord shut him in" (Genesis 7:16), so the masses of this world will not realize the Lord is coming until it is too late.

Just as the Sodomites would heed no warning of righteousness and continued to commit their gross immoralities until the very day God destroyed the cities with fire and brimstone, so will this generation and this age of our Lord's return be found unprepared.

I urge you today to accept my warning. The day of Christ is at hand. All these signposts and indications of the last days are what Jesus meant when He said, "As it was in the days of Noah and Lot, so shall it be in the days of the coming of the Son of man."

Are you prepared to meet God this moment? Are you ready? Open your heart to His Holy Spirit.

Let us pray.

> *Oh, our God, in these troubled, decadent times, when mankind has failed to honor You and has followed his own depraved heart, will You not awaken us anew to the coming judgments? Will You not stir us from our sleep that we might realize that as quickly as lightening shines from the east to the west, in the moment, in the twinkling of an eye, You are coming in clouds of glory for your own? That day will be one of lamentation and destruction for the wicked and unrepentant. Hear us today, our Father. We seek Your mercy and forgiveness. Number us with the righteous. Cover us with the grace and blood of Your Own dear Son. In His name we pray. Amen.*

When it is evening, ye say, It will be fair weather: for the sky is red. And in the morning, It will be foul weather to day: for the sky is red and lowring. O ye hypocrites, ye can discern the face of the sky; but can ye not discern the signs of the times?
(Matthew 16:2, 3).

8

The Trends of These Times

Introduction

A few years ago a cover page of *U.S. News and World Report* magazine bore the title, "Neither War Nor Peace, A Survey of Our Time." The article covered the political, economic, military and social developments of these times. It was a reminder that many in today's world are contemplating those various lessons to be drawn from a fair examination of these times.

Seaton Watson, the author of the above-mentioned article, gave much attention to the growth of communism since the end of World War II. He also commented on the Cold War between the West and the East, noting how radically our lives have been changed through the discovery and development of atomic weapons of mass destruction.

Our world had an abrupt awakening upon realizing these weapons could actually mean the end of life on this earth. Numerous quotes have highlighted the reality of modern life on the edge. One scientist said,

"We have discovered something with which we could destroy ourselves." Another called the atomic bomb a God-like chemical.

Winston Churchill said, "We have come to the end of our tether." And H.G. Wells noted, "The ship of civilization is sinking now."

Although our political leaders fine-tuned the doctrine of peaceful coexistence, and although the Berlin Wall came down in 1989—leading many to think we were on the verge of a new world—it has not happened.

Around the world are what leaders now call hot spots, and very few of us see the world as a safer place to live. Rather, every few weeks bring new challenges and new dangers from the threat of rogue nations and political terrorists, so much so that some theorize that our dangers are actually now worse than when we were paired off face-to-face with Communist block nations.

Caleb Carr, editor of *MHQ: The Quarterly Journal of Military History*, says, "We are, today, farther from a viable international order than we were fifty or even ten years ago, if only because there are fewer sound, powerful nations to support one."

These are indeed crisis days and ominous times. Fear so grips the whole human race that many people feel the question is not "How may we better our society?" but "Can we survive at all?"

Unforeseen Dangers

I read another article which was the result of an interview with the head of the U.S. Air Force. Although this man was a global strategist with many years' experience in defending our nation, he concluded there was never a more critical period in human history than now.

Strangely, though, while these days are filled with previously undreamed-of dangers, they were foretold by the apostle Paul in his letter to young Timothy.

> This know also, that in the last days perilous times shall come. For men shall be lovers of their own selves, covetous, boasters, proud, blasphemers, disobedient to parents, unthankful, unholy, Without natural affection, trucebreakers, false accusers, incontinent, fierce, despisers of those that are good, Traitors, heady, high minded, lovers of pleasures more than lovers of God; Having a form of godliness, but denying the power thereof: from such turn away (2 Timothy 3:1-5).

The word *perilous* in this first verse means dangerous. And verses two through five relate some of the dangers with which we have to cope in these last days.

Population Growth

Another trend causing world leaders a great deal of concern is population growth. We are told there are now 6 billion people living on earth. Newspapers recently carried headlines of the birth of a baby in India, number 1 billion for that nation alone.

The U.S. Census Bureau tells us it took from the dawn of human history until the year 1800 for earth's population to reach one billion. We reached a second billion souls on earth in 1920, a period of 120 years. It took only 40 years, however, to reach the third billion, in 1960; and 20 years to add a fourth. That was in 1980. In the two decades since, we have added two further billions to the population of the earth; and it is predicted that, in spite of some decline in the growth rate, there will be eight billion of us on this earth by the year 2026.

The concern of world leaders is from an economic, social and political point of view. Will we be able to feed these growing multitudes? What are these numbers going to do to our social structures, institutions and geographic boundaries? How is daily life going to be impacted? And what must we do to adjust?

But there is another population-related concern which bothers me even more than the economic and social impact of our numerical growth. What is the church doing? Are we taking the Great Commission as seriously as we ought?

Nationalism

Another trend of these times is the growth of nationalism, which is creating international strife and confusion, and is provoking racial hatred in many places.

Places like Kosovo and Bosnia have come center stage on the evening news, conjuring up ghosts of the past with such phrases as *ethnic cleansing* and *genocide.* Some of us thought the days of mass graves and the random killing of innocent people had passed, only to find our world once again in chaos.

Other groups of people within what we thought were well-established national borders—such as the Kurds in both Turkey and Iraq, and the Islamic rebels in Russia— are waging class warfare and creating havoc as never before, with no end in sight. This too must be viewed as a trend of the times worth noting.

Lack of Spiritual Sensitivity

These present happenings should provoke revival and righteousness. Instead they produce complacency and breed wickedness.

The prophet Isaiah's indictment against Israel for complacency and unconcern in a time of trouble could easily be brought against our nation today. "The ox knoweth his owner, and the ass his master's crib: but Israel doth not know, my people doth not consider" (Isaiah 1:3). In this passage more wisdom is attributed to the dumb beasts of the field than to the supposedly intelligent beings who do not know God as their owner.

Jeremiah echoed this same theme: "Yea, the stork in the heaven knoweth her appointed times; and the turtle and the crane and the swallow observe the time of their coming; but my people know not the judgment of the Lord" (Jeremiah 8:7).

It seems that all God's creation has done His bidding better than man. In the face of impending danger, man goes on unmoved.

A man who sits on the top council of the United States

THE RAPTURE AND REVELATION

government declares, "I hold the deepest pessimism concerning the nation's future."

We appear to lack interest in the life or death problems we face and appear to lack any other objective than that of making life easier and more enjoyable.

This has become the ease era that has given birth to a fat, opulent, ease-loving generation often chained to alcoholism and drug abuse, and fettered by fleshly habits they can little afford. This luxury-loving generation has produced over one million alcoholics that are institutionalized today. This is not to speak of the multitudes who are not in institutions.

Lovers of Pleasures

The apostle Paul reminded us of this trend of the times when he wrote, "Men shall be . . . lovers of pleasure more than lovers of God" (2 Timothy 3:2, 4).

Think about it.

- The Lord's day has been turned into a holiday rather than a holy day.

- People are eight times more likely to attend the movies than Sunday school.

- American families are spending many hours a week before their television sets.

- Sports stadiums are packed and nightclubs are bulging, while churches, for the most part, are comparatively empty.

- Prayer meeting service, where it still exists, is attended only by a faithful few.

- Less than 5 percent of Americans attend Sunday evening church services, while the other 95 percent either work, rest or go on a pleasure binge.

This self-indulgent generation has caused a combination of Sodom and Gomorrah, Rome and Babylon to be experienced in a single setting. In search of pleasure, they have allowed their lust to run wild. They can no longer be satisfied through the natural channels created by God, but must resort to unnatural affection. The Scripture says that men shall be "without natural affection" (v. 3). This simply means they cannot control themselves and their affections.

A Harvard professor has said, "Our civilization has become so preoccupied with sex that it now oozes from all the pores of American life." Moral standards are now being dragged through a sludge of filth.

Moral Depravity

I once read a newspaper article entitled, "Return to Old-Fashioned Moral Values." Surprisingly enough, these are the words of a movie star, Shirley Temple. The morals of this nation have worn threadbare and even non-religious people are crying out against the indecency of our time. Some newspapers refuse to accept ads for some of the modern movies.

Yet, there are those milk-and-water preachers who are proclaiming a whitewashed, rose water gospel that will not save.

How long can America stand with the heart of her nation putrefied and blackened by these sins? Shall not God visit us for these things? The moral depravity of our times is a greater threat to our destruction than nuclear weapons.

The whole trend of our times is toward this moral depravity. Lust is glorified. It dominates modern music. It is a must in the realm of modern advertisement and an ever-present evil in literature. Many nations who were otherwise unconquerable have fallen through inward moral decay.

The Bible warns that these times will be given over to total depravity. "Knowing this first, that there shall come in the last days scoffers, walking after their own lusts" (2 Peter 3:3); "Having eyes full of adultery, and that cannot cease from sin" (2:14). The whole atmosphere reeks with moral impurity.

The bulk of television programs and even commercials sink us into filth. No wonder many of us, after being immersed in this muck, come out feeling physically and morally dirty.

The smut traffic is a growing menace. Many believe the rise in juvenile delinquency and sex crimes can be traced directly to this proliferation of lewd, pornographic literature made available to our nation's youth. Some of it is under the guise of art and some under the guise of education, but this so-called literature inflames the passion and establishes new images in the minds of young people.

Christian principles of morality are viewed as obsolete and unsuited for this age and are replaced with a philosophy of "If it feels good, do it." If no harmful physical or psychological effects are apparent, then go ahead. It must be all right.

Social approval does not make a thing right. God has set standards of right and wrong. They are forever settled in the heavens. God is immutable and never changes. When this whole earth turns white from the heat of His judgment and cools into a cinder, His standards will still exist.

The Prevalence of Fear

This is a generation full of fear and anxiety. Murders, atrocities, and heinous crimes have become the order of the day. Fear has brought us despair and has girdled the globe with confusion and strife.

The Bible tells us, "Fear hath torment" (1 John 4:18); and people are tormented today because of failure to put faith in God.

The writer of Proverbs gave us an appropriate reminder, "The fear of man bringeth a snare: but whoso putteth his trust in the Lord shall be safe" (Proverbs 29:25).

The difficulty of our day is that men fear men but have no fear of God. As the Psalmist said, "The transgression of the wicked saith within my heart, that there is no fear of God before his eyes" (Psalm 36:1). If we put our trust in God, we need not fear man. Jesus said, "And fear not them which kill the body, but are not able to kill the soul: but rather fear him which is able to destroy both soul and body in hell" (Matthew 10:28).

The man who trusts in God has a refuge and a fortress. "There shall no evil befall thee, neither shall any plague come nigh thy dwelling. For he shall give his angels charge over thee, to keep thee in all thy ways" (Psalm 91:10, 11).

Men of these times are putting their faith in false security. They place their hope in stocks, bonds, securities, land and real estate, but nothing is sure other than Christ. In the words of the old song,

On Christ the solid rock I stand,
All other ground is sinking sand,
All other ground is sinking sand.

Years ago I read of what would happen if the cities of our world were subjected to a nuclear attack. The article revealed that the super H-bomb would blast a hole 3,800 feet deep and almost five miles wide. The probable form of attack would be two super H-bombs dropped on each major center. One would explode in the air, and the other would penetrate the earth to a depth of 50 or 60 feet, destroying underground structures over a radius of more than 30 miles. Can you imagine the devastation?

Conclusion

In light of the trends of these times, I want to ask you a sobering question. "Are you prepared to meet God?"

Do these times sober you and make you God-conscious, or are you taking advantage of these times to go deeper in sin? God's mercy will soon be turned into judgment. The Lamb of God will become as fierce as a lion. Now is your chance to repent while opportunity still lasts. This old world will fade. God's Word will last.

John reminds us, "The world passeth away and the lust thereof" (1 John 2:17).

Now is your opportunity for repentance, prayer and salvation.

While the tender voice of Christ still speaks and He still woos and calls you to come home, surrender your heart and let Jesus come into your life. Time is short. Your life is brief. Only a few more moments of time are left. Now is your time to say, "Jesus, come into my heart." Today is the day of salvation. Now is the accepted time.

Let us pray.

> *Dear God, draw those reading these words today to Your bleeding side. Open their hearts to the gentle touch of Your Spirit. Redeem them through faith in Your Son, Savior of the world. Shelter them in the hollow of Your hand and never let them stray—until the day you call them home. I pray in the name of Jesus Christ our Lord. Amen.*

For the children of Israel shall abide many days without a king, and without a prince, and without a sacrifice, and without an image, and without an ephod, and without teraphim: Afterward shall the children of Israel return, and seek the Lord their God, and David their king; and shall fear the Lord and his goodness in the latter days.
(Hosea 3:4, 5).

9

Israel: God's Time Clock

Introduction

Those who study Bible prophecy and realize the important role the Jews will play in the end time have chosen to call Israel the pointer on God's world clock, or God's time clock.

The eyes of the world are so focused on the Middle East, especially Israel, that it seems but natural to ask, "Why is everyone so concerned about a small strip of land called Israel?"

Along with many Bible scholars, I believe Israel *is* an historical barometer and there are prophecies yet to be fulfilled, events yet to occur on the world stage in which Israel will play a starring role.

Modern Israel is certainly not geographically impressive. Israel's shore-line is the eastern seaboard of the Mediterranean, and its territory extends northwards through the Golan Heights and southwards through the Negev to the Sinai peninsula. To the north is Lebanon, northeast is Syria, east is Jordan, while Egypt lies to the south.

Prior to the Six Day War of 1967 Israel's land area was 8,000 square miles, slightly larger than New Jersey, with 120 miles of sandy coast.

Once again the question, why so much attention to Israel, a small nation with a present population of 6.3 million people?

Few in the secular realm realize the importance of Israel but in the revealing light of Bible prophecy we can find an explanation.

The Jews in History

The Jewish people have played a prominent role in world history for almost 4,000 years. Although they have been dispersed among the nations, slaughtered by the millions, exiled from country after country, discriminated against and abused, they continue until this day.

Any other people, under similar circumstances, would most surely have been exterminated long ago. But today, by miracle of miracles, the Jews who were without a land, without a king and without a government for 1878 years have managed to survive. They have done so in spite of every onslaught of Satan and every diabolical plan that could be devised to exterminate them.

Any review of the history of the Jewish people will make the picture all the more vivid.

When Jerusalem was overthrown by the Roman army in A.D. 70, 1,100,000 Jews perished. Ninety-seven thousand more were captured, and in A.D. 145 over a half-million were slain.

Many Jews were killed during the Crusades. Hundreds of thousands of Jewish people were destroyed during the Spanish Inquisition. The Jewish people have been persecuted, imprisoned and slaughtered in France, in the Soviet Union and in other European nations. In what is regarded as the worst of all modern atrocities, 6 million Jews were killed by the Nazis in Germany and in conquered areas such as Poland during World War II.

On May 31, 1962, after a long and well-publicized trial, Israeli authorities hanged Adolf Eichmann in punishment for his concentration camp activities during the Holocaust. That event was not without significance in these last days. It should make the world, especially Christian believers, more conscious of the fact that God's time clock is ticking toward the ominous hour of twelve. We are approaching the crisis hour. When God's time clock strikes twelve, this day will be finished and a new day will dawn.

Every time I visit the Middle East, I become more convinced we are living on the brink of the soon return of the Lord Jesus Christ. The Bible tells us,

> Now learn a parable of the fig tree; when his branch is yet tender, and putteth forth leaves, ye know that summer is nigh; So likewise ye, when ye shall see all these things, know that it is near, even at the doors. Verily I say unto you, This generation shall not pass, till all these things be fulfilled (Matthew 24:32-34).

The fig tree is symbolic of Israel, telling us that when Israel begins to bud and to put forth, we have an indication, a sign, the coming of the Lord is near. So far as I am concerned, this is the reason for all the feverish activity in the Middle East and for the worldwide attention being paid to the problems of that area.

The fulfillment of prophecy leading up to the dawn of the 21st century is indication of how quickly we are moving to the hour of Christ's soon return.

Pieces of the Puzzle

In 1917 when General Edmund Allenby led the British army in running the Turks out of Palestine, the prophecy concerning Israel suddenly took on new light. Dr. Chaim Weizmann, president of the World Scientist Movement, requested of Great Britain an officially recognized homeland of the Jews in Palestine.

On November 2, 1917, the historic Balfour Declaration was issued: "His Majesty's Government view with favour the establishment in Palestine of a national home for the Jewish people, and will use their best endeavours to facilitate the achievement of this object."

To add importance to this declaration, the League of Nations put their stamp of approval upon it and recognized the historic connection of the Jewish people and Palestine. Britain was given a mandate over Palestine. A new day had dawned for the Jews, though not without difficulty.

The Balfour Declaration encouraged a new wave of immigration. From all over Europe, Jews began a trek to their ancient homeland. The dead bones of Ezekiel had begun to stir and come together.

God had used the vision of dry bones coming to life to symbolize the return of Israel and the resurrection of the nation. These are the exact words:

> Thus saith the Lord God unto these bones; Behold, I will cause breath to enter into you, and ye shall live. . . . So I prophesied as he commanded me, and the breath came into them, and they lived, and stood up upon their feet, an exceeding great army (Ezekiel 37:5, 10).

The Word of God clearly sets forth the restoration of the Jews in the latter days. Here are three quotes from three separate Old Testament prophets:

> For the children of Israel shall abide many days without a king, and without a prince, and without a sacrifice, and without an image, and without an ephod, and without teraphim: Afterward shall the children of Israel return, and seek the Lord their God, and David their king; and shall fear the Lord and his goodness in the latter days (Hosea 3:4, 5).

> For I will take you from among the heathen, and gather you out of all countries, and will bring you into your own land (Ezekiel 36:24).

> Behold, I will gather them out of all countries, whither I have driven them in mine anger, and in my fury, and in great wrath; and I will bring them

again unto this place, and I will cause them to dwell safely (Jeremiah 32:37).

As I see the pointer of God's world clock moving toward the midnight hour, my heart seems to beat faster, and I lift my head just a little higher, for I realize God's Word says, "When these things begin to come to pass, then look up, and lift your heads; for your redemption draweth nigh" (Luke 21:28). These words were spoken by our Lord Jesus Christ in connection with the return of Israel.

The Mid-East Conflict

Although the leading powers of the world have recognized the Jewish claim to Palestine, it has been evident from the beginning that the Arabs were determined to see that Israel would never become a state. This rivalry between Arabs and Jews traces back to the day Ishmael was born, son of Abraham by his handmaid Hagar. It is the traditional strife between Isaac and Ishmael—Isaac the Jew and Ishmael the Arab.

Regardless of the circumstances, the inspired Word of God is going to be fulfilled in every detail.

Note these words of the prophet Isaiah,

> Who hath heard such a thing? who hath seen such things? Shall the earth be made to bring forth in one day? or shall a nation be born at once? for as soon as Zion travailed, she brought forth her children. Shall I bring to the birth, and not cause to bring forth? saith

the Lord: shall I cause to bring forth, and shut the womb? saith thy God. Rejoice ye with Jerusalem, and be glad with her, all ye that love her: rejoice for joy with her, all ye that mourn for her: That ye may suck, and be satisfied with the breasts of her consolations; that ye may milk out, and be delighted with the abundance of her glory. For thus saith the Lord, Behold, I will extend peace to her like a river, and the glory of the Gentiles like a flowing stream: then shall ye suck, ye shall be borne upon her sides, and be dandled upon her knees. As one whom his mother comforteth, so will I comfort you; and ye shall be comforted in Jerusalem (Isaiah 66:8-13).

On November 29, 1947, the United Nations assembly approved that Palestine should be partitioned into two states, one Jewish and one Arab, with an economic union between them. The city of Jerusalem was to be internationalized. The Jews accepted this offer, but the Arabs did not.

Would the Jews declare themselves a state in the face of the threat of all their enemies? That was the question. The world stood by with hands off while the Arabs attacked Palestine in an effort to crush the new nation. The Palestinian Arabs and the armies of Egypt, Syria, Lebanon, Jordan, Saudi Arabia, Sudan—all joined in the attack.

At that time Israel had only 35,000 partially trained troops. Their total armament consisted of a few thousand rifles, some homemade guns, a few hundred machine guns, and a few "Yankee" aircraft guns and mortars. With only 600,000 people, the little country was surrounded on three sides with no place to retreat except into the sea. Nevertheless, through a miracle of God, the young Jewish nation survived.

Another very obvious miracle of survival took place two decades later. Following months of conflict between Israel and Syria in which Israeli tanks crossed into Syria and Israeli Mirage fighters shot down six Syrian MIG-21 fighters, the Six-Day Arab-Israeli War began on June 5, 1967.

Against unbelievable odds, Israeli jets and armor aborted an Arab invasion of Israel. Egyptian and Syrian air forces, whose equipment had been supplied largely by Moscow, were totally demolished. And, on June 7, the Israelis took Arab Jerusalem, incorporating it with the rest of the city on June 27, guaranteeing freedom of access to the Holy Places for people of all faiths.

As a result of this war, Israel has retained most of the strategic conquered areas, which along with Arab Jerusalem contain half the population of Jordan and half her economic resources. This is the backdrop for the continuing conflicts between Israel and her Arab neighbors.

Prophecy Fulfilled

Just before the dawning of the Jewish Sabbath, at four o'clock in the afternoon on May 14, 1948, a few hours after the British had officially withdrawn, the founding fathers of Israel met in the Tel Aviv Art Museum. David Ben-Gurion, the prime minister, read the Declaration of Independence.

Israel then occupied 80 percent of Palestine and still had an Arab population of 200,000, after 500,000 had fled. The new state opened its doors to Jews from all over the world.

On that day, a nation was born. That day Israel become a state and prophecy was fulfilled.

While the world looked on, many of us Christians looked up. We knew the event was another indication that Jesus Christ could come at any moment.

Ben-Gurion stood and read these words,

> The land of Israel was the birthplace of the Jewish people. Here their spiritual, religious and national identity was formed. Here they achieved independence and created a culture of national and universal significance. Here they wrote and gave the Bible to the world.

He continued by saying that the State of Israel was to be opened for the ingathering of the exiled. It was to be based on liberty, justice and peace, as taught by the Hebrew prophets.

The whole world was electrified when it realized a nation was born out of antiquity, one that had been dead for 1878 years.

Following this declaration, the National Anthem was played. The flag of the world's youngest state was raised. As it was unfurled, the blue and white colors of the flag symbolized the robe worn by Israel's high priest when he entered the holy temple on the Day of Atonement. The six-pointed star, or the Star of David, is said to have decorated David's shield.

THE RAPTURE AND REVELATION

Yes, a nation had been born in a day. God's prophetic Word had come to pass.

The Continuing Drama

The winning of the War of Independence against unthinkable odds and the conflicts since have all been an indication that God's Word will always prevail, even if God has to perform a miracle to carry it out.

Three times daily, for hundreds of years, Jews throughout the world had prayed toward Jerusalem to the chant of this prayer, "Sound the great trumpet for our freedom. Raise the banner for gathering our exiles. And gather us together from the four corners of the earth into our own land."

On that day—the day that Israel was declared a state—the population was only 600,000. Today Jews from all over the world have returned and the population has soared to almost six and a half million.

The Scripture says, "And he shall set up an ensign for the nations, and shall assemble the outcasts of Israel, and gather together the dispersed of Judah from the four corners of the earth" (Isaiah 11:12). In fulfillment of this prophecy, Jews have come from at least 72 different countries, from different civilizations, different cultures and even different centuries.

An example of what I mean by different centuries is the return of Ethiopian Jews who have come to Israel after living in such primitive conditions that they had never seen a water faucet, a modern fork or spoon or tin can.

In a move called "Operation Magic Carpet," 50,000 of these Jews were airlifted into Israel. Others have come since. Although these people had never seen an airplane, they had been told of Isaiah's prophecies which stated, "They that wait upon the Lord shall renew their strength; they shall mount up with wings as eagles" (Isaiah 40:31); and, "Who are these that fly as a cloud, and as the doves to their windows?" (60:8).

With these Scriptures in mind, they saw giant airplanes and realized they were to return to their homeland. They climbed on board with hope.

The saga of Jews returning to their ancient homeland continues, a great number from the former Soviet Union and some still from Ethiopia. An article in *USA Today,* May 16, 2000, titled, "Ethiopian Jews fight for the opportunity to emigrate to Israel," detailed the living conditions and Jewish faith of thousands in Ethiopia still trying to get to Israel.

I visited Israel in 1952, the year of her first harvest, and again in May 1961. In just that short span of time, I was amazed at the swamps and deserts that had been transformed into fertile fields, beautiful vineyards and orange groves. The Plain of Sharon again had blossomed like a rose. The prophecy is fulfilled: "Israel shall blossom and bud, and fill the face of the world with fruit" (Isaiah 27:6).

At almost every turn of the road I was made conscious that the coming of the Lord draws near. In talking with the Jewish people, I did not find one who was not looking for Messiah to return. In Israel today there seems to be a consciousness that the hour will be soon. Although they are not looking for Jesus to come again, they do seem to realize that someone is coming. Something significantly important is about to happen.

Recently, I visited in Jerusalem and banners were displayed in several places. I asked a Jewish friend what the banners said. He replied, "The Messiah is coming." I told him I was also looking for the Messiah, but I was looking for Him to come the second time. His response was, "When the Messiah does come I am going to ask Him, 'Is this Your first visit to Jerusalem?'"

Conclusion

I am confident the coming of the Lord draws nigh. Now is the time to prepare your heart to meet Jesus Christ.

At any moment, at any hour, Jesus Christ could appear in the clouds of glory. This is only one of the many evidences in the world today. "So I prophesied as he commanded me, and the breath came into them, and they lived, and stood up upon their feet, an exceeding great army" (Ezekiel 37:10).

Should Jesus Christ come today, should He come now in the next twenty-four hours, would you be ready to meet Him?

You may scoff at the thought of Israel being God's prophetic time clock, but remember, His Word is always true.

The coming of the Lord draws near. Be patient and establish your heart. The Lord is at hand.

Let us pray.

Father in heaven, in faith we look up, knowing our redemption draws near, and the time for our Lord's return is upon us. Be gracious and merciful to those not yet prepared. Touch them with Your convicting Holy Spirit and draw them to Your truth. Grant each of us the spiritual wisdom which understands You come first in our lives. For thine is the Kingdom, now and forever. Amen.

Evil men and seducers shall wax worse and
worse, deceiving, and being deceived
(2 Timothy 3:13).

Clouds they are without water, carried
about of winds
(Jude 12) .

Sensual, having not the Spirit
(Jude 19).

Raging waves of the sea, foaming
out their own shame
(Jude 13).

Ever learning, and never able to
come to the knowledge of the truth
(2 Timothy 3:7).

They shall turn away their ears from the truth,
and shall be turned unto fables
(2 Timothy 4:4).

10

Spiritual Conditions of the Last Days

Introduction

The terms "latter times," "the time of the end," "the last time" and "the last day," are used throughout the Word of God to indicate a period prior to the second coming of the Lord Jesus Christ. The Word of God is very clear concerning many things which will happen in these last days. The political and economic conditions of the last days are foretold. Technological and scientific achievements are set forth in no uncertain terms. The moral and spiritual life in the last days is vividly pictured. I will not be able to discuss all these various phases, but I would like to focus on the spiritual conditions of the last days.

A prominent statesman once said that the whole current of contemporary history seems to indicate a climax in the near future. It is expected no less by those who view the panorama from a materialistic or rationalistic standpoint than by those who endeavor to read the signs of the times in light of God's Word. The whole world stands in anxiety, harassed by fear, asking, "What will happen next?"

At the same time, while our eyes are focused on world conditions, distress of nations, international conflict, political issues and technological progress, most people are unaware of, and unconcerned about, what is happening in the spiritual world.

Spiritual Apostasy

The New Testament declares there will be a general apostasy in the last days. The Bible says, "Let no man deceive you by any means: for that day shall not come, except there come a falling away first" (2 Thessalonians 2:3). This apostasy does not mean merely backsliding, for one can stray from Christ and not become apostate. *Apostasy* means the abandonment of faith—"Now the Spirit speaketh expressly, that in the latter times some shall depart from the faith, giving heed to seducing spirits, and doctrines of devils" (1 Timothy 4:1).

This widespread apostasy began not with attack from without, but from within. In the theological seminaries and pulpits of our day, the cardinal principles of God's Word have been undermined. The old songs of the blood have been called nonsensical, foolish hymns. Church officials have denounced the Virgin Birth, the substitutionary atonement, the bodily resurrection of Jesus Christ, and the Second Coming. They declare there is no personal devil and they have instituted an amoral, totally human-ethic religion.

This generation has rationalized faith until it has removed from the gospel message every vital quality and its miracle-working power. Deep spirituality has been exchanged for vague religiousness, without a definite born-again experience with God. Sound doctrine has become a matter of scorn; and multitudes of people who were at one time beaming, glowing Christians now seem to express little or no interest in true religion at all. Many have literally turned their backs on God.

The Bible tells us,

> For the time will come when they will not endure sound doctrine; but after their own lusts shall they heap to themselves teachers, having itching ears; And they shall turn away their ears from the truth, and shall be turned unto fables (2 Timothy 4:3, 4).

Even Christ in His Mount Olive discourse warned us of the deception of these days, "And many false prophets shall rise, and shall deceive many" (Matthew 24:11).

False Religions

When churches become spiritually dead, members starve for spiritual food. They become fertile soil in which false religion can take root. The world is hungering for inner satisfaction, and this is the reason for the growth of cults in these last days. When men depart from the faith, the Bible says they will give heed to seducing spirits or deceiving spirits and the doctrine of devils.

Since man is innately religious, the spirit within him cries for something to worship. His search for satisfaction has often caused him to be deceived and to fall prey to false doctrine. This is the reason Jesus gave warning, "Take heed that no man deceive you" (Matthew 24:4). John the

Beloved wrote, "Many deceivers are entered into the world, who confess not that Jesus Christ is come in the flesh. This is a deceiver and an antichrist" (2 John: 7). And Paul declares, "Evil men and seducers shall wax worse and worse, deceiving, and being deceived" (2 Timothy 3:13).

The apostle Peter gives us a stark warning I want to pass along:

> But there were false prophets also among the people, even as there shall be false teachers among you, who privily shall bring in damnable heresies, even denying the Lord that bought them, and bring upon themselves swift destruction (2 Peter 2:1).

Notice, Peter forewarns us of those false prophets who deny the blood, the purchase price of Calvary.

Jude speaks in similar tones, referring to false prophets as: "Clouds they are without water, carried about of winds" (Jude 12); "sensual, having not the Spirit" (v. 19); and "raging waves of the sea, foaming out their own shame" (v. 13).

As the time of the end draws nearer, more and more we shall see the feverish activity of false religions at work. Widespread ignorance of God's Word also accounts for the rapid growth of false religions. In this age of intellect and reason, when the world is more literate than in any period of human history, men are ignorant of the truth. The Word of God says, "This know also, that in the last days perilous times shall come" (2 Timothy 3:1). Men shall be "Ever learning, and never able to come to the knowledge of the truth" (v. 7). "They shall turn away their ears from the truth, and shall be turned unto fables" (4:4).

Listen to the words of the prophet Amos, words surely

applicable to our day, "Behold, the days come saith the Lord God, that I will send a famine in the land, not a famine of bread, nor a thirst for water, but of the hearing the words of the Lord" (Amos 8:11). That time of famine, that time of spiritual hunger and thirst is now upon us. There was a day when most churches taught the Bible. Those who attended meetings had some Bible background and spiritual knowledge. The Word of God was read and taught in the public schools and around the family altar. This background for spiritual knowledge made it easier for the evangelist to reap a spiritual harvest. But there is a lack of a Biblical background among people of the world today which makes it increasingly more difficult for evangelistic campaigns to be conducted successfully.

Instead of the Word of God being preached, taught, read and believed, the Word is being criticized in schools, pulpits, colleges and even in the homes. The Word of God upon which our nation was founded has now become an offense to the people. When God's Word becomes an offense to us, a curse rests upon us and we bring all of the plagues and the judgments of God's Book down upon our shoulders. This places us in a precarious condition, for God cannot favor those who willfully deny Him.

Deception

The devil has deceived people into believing some type of religion is better than no religion at all. Therefore, many have adopted the philosophy that it makes no difference what you believe just so you believe in something.

I want to give you some scriptures of warning:

"Let no man deceive himself" (1 Corinthians 3:18).

"There is a way which seemeth right unto a man, but the end thereof are the ways of death" (Proverbs 14:12).

The key phrase here is "seemeth right." But the end is death.

It is not enough to be religious. One can have vain religion. The Marxist-Leninist theory of Communism is a religion, but it failed socially and did not even pretend to have power to save eternally.

For life eternal, every individual must have a personal encounter with the Lord Jesus Christ.

Christ has declared there is only one way. There are not many routes, all leading to heaven. There is only one route. Jesus said, "I am the way, the truth, and the life: no man cometh unto the Father, but by me" (John 14:6). Further, "Strait is the gate, and narrow is the way, which leadeth unto life, and few there be that find it" (Matthew 7:14).

Paul tells us there is, "One Lord, one faith, one baptism, One God and Father of all, who is above all, and through all, and in you all" (Ephesians 4:5, 6).

The idea that God has placed many religions and beliefs in the world so that people can believe almost anything and live almost any way and still make it to heaven is but a subtle doctrine of the devil that damns the souls of men. There is only one way. Any man that climbs up any other way, the Bible says, the same is a thief and a robber (John 10:1).

Formality

Another prevailing condition in these last days is the formality of churches. This is one of the basic difficulties in Evangelicalism. Our churches are so cold, lifeless and dead. The altars are barren. It is true that the churches are filled with activity, but where are these active people on prayer meeting night? It takes a movie, a party or a social to attract some people to church. There is no doubt about what Paul meant when he said, "Having a form of godliness, but denying the power thereof" (2 Timothy 3:5).

The form of religion increases, while religion itself becomes more and more powerless. Formality breeds indifference, lukewarmness and worldliness and is a fertile field in which false religion can grow. The church of Laodicea is a portrait of some of today's churches. God's charge was that they were neither cold nor hot. From all indications Laodicea was a progressive church. The people there were rich and increased in goods. Their testimony was "We have need of nothing." They were organizationally correct. They were making material gains and had the appearance of success. But God looked at them and said, "Because thou art lukewarm, and neither cold nor hot, I will spue thee out of my mouth. . . . Thou art wretched, and miserable, and poor, and blind, and naked" (Revelation 3:16, 17).

These are days when successes are determined by material gains, programs and financial drives. As essential as such things are, they can only serve as vehicles to carry the gospel. When they become anything other than that, they become accursed. The forces of formalism have stifled religious conviction, paralyzed the nerve center of the church and drained men of their compassion for the lost. It has caused churches to be relegated to mere social clubs and service centers rather than great evangelistic centers where the lost can find their way out of darkness into marvelous light.

Worldliness

Where there is formal religion only, there will be no resistance to worldliness. The spirit of the age has eaten its way into the church like a cancerous growth and has left the church pale and anemic, without energy to resist the attractions of the world.

Judged by the way people live, it is hard to tell the difference between church members and sinners of today. So many church members have given themselves over to almost every form of worldly indulgence until there is no longer a clear line of demarcation between the church and the world. No wonder so many have strayed from the house of God! No wonder that, in many quarters, the church no longer has the magnetic drawing power which God intended it to have.

The church, like Israel, has changed its glory for that which doth not profit. This formality, lukewarmness and lethargy is set forth in the parable of the ten virgins, five of whom were wise and five foolish.

What was the difference?

They all had lamps. They all took their lamps with them. They were all virgins. They all had the appearance of readiness. But when the cry was made, "Behold, the bridegroom cometh; go ye out to meet him" (Matthew 25:6), it was discovered the foolish virgins had no oil in their lamps. They had form, but no fire. They had the appearance, but no substance. They had the religious exercise, but no reality.

The story ends in a sad note. While the foolish virgins went to buy oil, the bridegroom came. They that were ready went in with him to the marriage, and the door was shut. The other virgins came saying, "Lord, Lord, open to us." He answered and said, "Verily I say unto you, I know you not" (vv. 11, 12).

Could it be possible that you are going through the motions of religion, living under the shelter of the church, maybe even belonging to the church, active in the church . . . and yet . . . not prepared to meet Jesus Christ?

Conclusion

I ask you to examine yourself today in light of the fact that the midnight cry will soon be given. Only those who are ready will be saved and admitted to the Marriage Supper of the Lamb.

I want you to be in that number. God wishes the same. That is why He has loved you so, and given His Son for your salvation and deliverance.

Let us pray.

> *Almighty God, we are a fortunate generation, living in the last days, and perhaps even destined to behold Christ's return. We rejoice in our hope and in our conviction that Your Word is infallible. Thank You for the grace and mercy that makes this hope a living reality. It is not true with all our neighbors. Not true with many in this generation. So we pray for them. Be near them. Touch them. Draw them to the glory of the Cross and the perfect love of Your Son. In His name we pray. Amen.*

*And he gathered them together into a place
called in the Hebrew tongue Armageddon.
And the seventh angel poured out his vial
into the air; and there came a great voice out
of the temple of heaven, from the throne,
saying, It is done. And there were voices, and
thunders, and lightnings; and there was
a great earthquake, such as was not since men
were upon the earth, so mighty an earthquake,
and so great. And the great city was divided
into three parts, and the cities of the nations
fell: and great Babylon came in
remembrance before God, to give unto her
the cup of the wine of the
fierceness of his wrath*
(Revelation 16:16-19).

11

The Battle of Armageddon

Introduction

The word *Armageddon* has been used frequently in recent years. Not many people are aware of the true meaning of Armageddon. However, they are aware that it represents some terrible event. Satan's long course of rebellion and working against God will climax in the Battle of Armageddon.

The latter part of the Tribulation period, called the Great Tribulation, will be filled with war and unbelievable judgments upon the earth. The Battle of Armageddon will conclude the Great Tribulation period. This battle will be Satan's last attempt to subjugate and to exterminate the Jews. It must be remembered that at that time, the Jews will be at peace in their own land because of a covenant with the Antichrist who is an enemy of God.

The Antichrist, having broken his covenant with the Jews and having received the approval of the world, marshals all the military forces and combines the armies of the world to move against Jerusalem. Never has such an army been seen in all the world. Never has there been such a magnificent display of power controlled by one man. But while the nations of the world are being gathered together in the Middle East for the final battle called Armageddon, the Lord Jesus Christ, with His armies in glory and the angels of heaven, stands poised for the Great Revelation, known as the Second Coming of the Lord Jesus Christ.

The Antichrist, who receives his power from Satan and who takes the place of God, has set himself up as God and prepares to fight against the Almighty God.

The Revelation

The revelation must be distinguished from the translation or Rapture of the church. At the Rapture of the church, the saints of God will be caught away to meet the Lord in the air before the Tribulation period; but the second coming of Christ, or the revelation of Jesus Christ, will take place at the end of the Tribulation period when Christ shall come back to this earth.

Zechariah describes this event,

> Then shall the Lord go forth, and fight against those nations, as when he fought in the day of battle. And his feet shall stand in that day upon the mount of Olives, which is before Jerusalem on the east, and the mount of Olives shall cleave in the midst thereof toward the east and toward the west, and there shall be a very great valley; and half of the mountain shall remove toward the north, and half of it toward the south (Zechariah 14:3, 4).

This Second Coming is also described by John the Revelator:

> And I saw heaven opened, and behold a white horse; and he that sat upon him was called Faithful and True, and in righteousness he doth judge and make war. His eyes were as a flame of fire, and on his head were many crowns; and he had a name written, that no man knew, but he himself. And he was clothed with a vesture dipped in blood: and his name is called The Word of God. And the armies which were in heaven followed him upon white horses, clothed in fine linen, white and clean. And out of his mouth goeth a sharp sword, that with it he should smite the nations: and he shall rule them with a rod of iron: and he treadeth the winepress of the fierceness and wrath of Almighty God (Revelation 19:11-15).

When Jesus Christ comes again for the saints, the time of the Rapture, He will appear in the heavens and the saints will be caught up to meet the Lord in the air. When He comes at the revelation, He will return to earth with His saints. At His first appearing, which is for His church, not everyone will hear His call, for only believers will see Him.

But when Jesus comes back with His saints, the Word of God tells us everyone shall behold Him. "Behold, he cometh with clouds; and every eye shall see him, and they also which pierced him: and all kindreds of the earth shall wail because of him" (Revelation 1:7).

Those that pierced Him shall look upon Him. They shall ask, ". . . What are these wounds in thine hands?

Then he shall answer, Those with which I was wounded in the house of my friends" (Zechariah 13:6).

This revelation will not be a coming of humiliation and grace. It will be a coming of glory. He will not come as a lamb, but as a lion. He will not come for the salvation of humanity, but as a judge of all the world.

Coming of a Conqueror

While the conquering powers of the Antichrist are reveling in their victory and gloating over their strength, while the whole world in awe wonders about the Beast and bows prostrate at his feet, the sun is suddenly darkened. The moon fails to give her light. Stars begin to fall from heaven and all the powers of heaven tremble.

The Bible says,

> Immediately after the tribulation of those days shall the sun be darkened, and the moon shall not give her light, and the stars shall fall from heaven, and the powers of the heavens shall be shaken: And then shall appear the sign of the Son of man in heaven: and then shall all the tribes of the earth mourn, and they shall see the Son of man coming in the clouds of heaven with power and great glory (Matthew 24:29, 30).

The light of the Antichrist is eclipsed by another light. The Sun of Righteousness has arisen with healing in His wings and the Day Star brightens the heavens with all of His glory. While the sun veils her face and the moon refuses to shine, the entire heavens and the whole earth are enveloped with the light of the coming of the Son of man.

The Bible says, "For as the lightning cometh out of the east, and shineth even unto the west; so shall also the coming of the Son of man be"(v. 27). As the appearance of the rainbow in the heavens, so is the brightness of the appearance of the glory of the Lord (Ezekiel 1:28). His eyes are shining like flames of fire. The brilliance increases and the eyes of the world rivet upon this spectacle of glory.

He comes with the clouds. He is attended by angels of glory and is surrounded by the saints of God. Enoch, the seventh from Adam, prophesied, "Behold, the Lord cometh with ten thousands of his saints" (Jude 14).

The Manner of His Coming

The heavens will light up with the glory of the Lord, the Lord descending with bright clouds, surrounded by angelic armies and accompanied by the saints of glory robed in dazzling garments. In this manner, Christ will descend to meet His foe. He will descend sitting upon a white horse, an emblem of His purity and holiness.

This will be a stark contrast to His first coming and life upon earth. At His triumphal entry into Jerusalem, Jesus Christ rode a borrowed donkey. He will come next time with majesty and glory, riding upon a white horse. He will come to judge in righteousness and to make war on the earth. The Prince of Peace and the Man who brought peace to a sin-sick world will then express His anger against the hosts of Satan. Men will realize the Lord is a God of battle, a God of justice, a Holy Man of war.

Instead of a crown of thorns upon His head, there will be many crowns of gold which signify His authority. He will come as a mighty conqueror, the King of Kings and the Lord of Lords. He will smite the nations with a sword that goeth out of His mouth. Those who would not accept the sword of the spirit for the salvation of their souls will then be smitten by the sword of wrath. "But with righteousness shall he judge the poor, and reprove with equity for the meek of the earth: and he shall smite the earth with the rod of his mouth, and with the breath of his lips shall he slay the wicked" (Isaiah 11:4). The Bible says, "And out of his mouth goeth a sharp sword, that with it he should smite the nations" (Revelation 19:15). He comes with great armies of saints in glory to rule the earth with a rod of iron. The people of the earth wail because of Him. They realize that they crucified the Lord of glory and they rejected their Messiah.

The Defeat of Antichrist

When the Antichrist sees this appearance of the Son of Man, he will make war against Him. "And I saw the beast, and the kings of the earth, and their armies, gathered together to make war against him that sat on the horse, and against his army" (v. 19).

Satan rallies the Antichrist to gather the forces of earth against the hosts of heaven. The kings of the earth and all their armies make war against the King of Kings and the Lord of Lords.

The time has come that man must realize God rules in the kingdom of men.

With one word from the lips of the King, the armies of this world will perish.

The Beast and the False Prophet will be taken and cast alive into the lake of fire. Dead bodies will be left as a feast for the birds and the fowls of the air. According to the Word of God,

> The people that have fought against Jerusalem; Their flesh shall consume away while they stand upon their feet, and their eyes shall consume away in their holes, and their tongue shall consume away in their mouth (Zechariah 14:12).

Simultaneously, an angel from heaven will put Satan under arrest and cast him into the bottomless pit where he will be sentenced for a thousand years (Revelation 20:1-3).

After Christ shall have conquered the Antichrist and Satan has been bound, those who were beheaded for the Word of God during the Tribulation period and for the testimony of Jesus Christ will be raised to life again. "And they lived and reigned with Christ a thousand years" (v. 4).

This is the completion of the First Resurrection (v. 5). This is called the gleaning of the First Resurrection. From this time onward, none of the followers of the Lord Jesus Christ will die.

The only resurrection to follow will be the Second Resurrection, or the Resurrection of the Unjust who will be brought before the Great White Throne Judgment.

The truth of this resurrection can be better understood by the Scripture, "But every man in his own order: Christ the firstfruits; afterward they that are Christ's at his coming" (1 Corinthians 15:23).

Notice the three phases of the First Resurrection: (1) Christ the firstfruits; (2) afterwards, they that are Christ's at his coming; and (3) they that are beheaded for the witness of Jesus. This is the First Resurrection. Many theologians have compared it to a harvest: the firstfruits, the great ingathering and the gleaning.

Then will follow the judgment of the living nations (Matthew 25:46). These nations shall be judged according to their treatment of the Jews, God's chosen people. This is not a general judgment of all righteous and wicked. After this judgment shall come to pass the fulfillment of the prayer in Matthew 6:10 that we are taught to pray:

> Thy kingdom come.
> Thy will be done in earth,
> As it is in heaven.

Jesus and His saints shall rule upon this earth and "The kingdoms of this world are become the kingdoms of our Lord, and of His Christ; and he shall reign for ever and ever" (Revelation 11:15).

Conclusion

With God's grace and help, I plan to be on the winning side when Armageddon arrives. I plan to be with the victorious saints, following in the wake of the Lord of Glory. I am striving to make my calling and election sure, through faith in His name.

What about you? What is your status with the Lord? Have you accepted Him as your Savior and Redeemer; or, are you still in rebellion?

Come to Him now. Ask God to forgive your sins. Bow your will and give your heart to Him. His Holy Spirit is with you. The Lord beckons with open arms.

Let us pray.

Our Father and our God, hear us today, for we are in desperate need. Our sins are more than we can handle but You have promised forgiveness. We seek that forgiveness in the name of Jesus Christ our Lord. We seek that forgiveness now, admitting our sins, our rebellious nature, and our helplessness. Grant us Your mercy, deliver us from the coming horror of the end time, and grant us a place in Your kingdom of righteousness. In Jesus name we pray. Amen.

*And I saw an angel come down from heaven,
having the key of the bottomless pit and
a great chain in his hand. And he laid hold
on the dragon, that old serpent, which is the
Devil, and Satan, and bound him a thousand
years. And cast him into the bottomless
pit, and shut him up, and set a seal upon him,
that he should deceive the nations no more,
till the thousand years should be fulfilled*
(Revelation 20:1-3).

12

The Reign of Peace

Introduction

The human race has thought about, and dreamed of, a perfect age since being driven from the paradise of Eden. Men have endeavored to achieve such an end, to create or build such a civilization by various methods, only to fail woefully.

The Greeks thought they could produce a superior race and finally evolve into a Utopian society. Others have theorized that the world will continually get better until we will move into a golden age here on earth. Such dreams and goals are contradicted by what the Bible says. The Bible speaks not of earthly paradise but of an end to history within the framework of "perilous times." Paul tells us, "Evil men and seducers shall wax worse and worse, deceiving, and being deceived" (2 Timothy 3:13).

The opposite of paradise is promised in God's Word. When men will look for "Peace and safety; then sudden destruction cometh upon them, as travail upon a woman with child; and they shall not escape" (1 Thessalonians 5:3). War, bloodshed, violence, drunkenness, immorality and many other vices will be the order of the day.

While it may be argued that scientifically and materially the world is getting better, the world continues to grow worse spiritually and morally.

A Coming Kingdom

The Word of God tells us there is coming a day when Christ shall set up a kingdom of righteousness on the earth. That is when the prayer that has been prayed by the church for nearly 2,000 years will be fulfilled—"Thy kingdom come. Thy will be done in earth, as it is in heaven" (Matthew 6:10).

This is a prayer lifted high in thousands of churches almost every Sunday morning the world over, but it is not prayed in vain. The prophet Daniel foresaw what was to happen and wrote about it.

> And in the days of these kings shall the God of heaven set up a kingdom, which shall never be destroyed: and the kingdom shall not be left to other people, but it shall break in pieces and consume all these kingdoms, and it shall stand for ever (Daniel 2:44).

This new kingdom will be ushered in by the Second Coming of the Lord Jesus Christ or the revelation of Christ with His saints, as recorded in the Book of Revelation:

> And I saw heaven opened, and behold a white horse; and he that sat upon him was called Faithful and True, and in righteousness he doth judge and make war. His eyes were as a flame of fire, and on his head were many crowns; and he had a name written, that no man knew, but he himself. And he

was clothed with a vesture dipped in blood: and his name is called The Word of God. And the armies which were in heaven followed him upon white horses, clothed in fine linen, white and clean. And out of his mouth goeth a sharp sword, that with it he should smite the nations: and he shall rule them with a rod of iron (Revelation 19:11-15).

The Revelation

When the Lord comes to establish His kingdom upon the earth, He will come with power and great glory; and, at this time, the great Battle of Armageddon will be fought. Before the Lord's kingdom can be established, however, the Antichrist must be destroyed. Paul tells us how that will take place: "The Lord shall consume [him] with the spirit of his mouth, and shall destroy with the brightness of his coming" (2 Thessalonians 2:8).

The first time Jesus Christ our Lord appeared on earth, as a baby born in Bethlehem, He came in humility and quietness. But the second time He appears, He will come with a shout from the vaulted domes of glory. The first time He came in lowliness; but the second time He will come with power and great glory. The first time, He came as the Lamb of God. When He comes again, He will come as King of Kings and Lord of Lords. The first time, He came as the sin-bearer; the second time He will appear without sin unto salvation.

The first time Jesus came He was despised and rejected. The second time He will rule in authority. The first time He bore a cross. The next time He will wear a golden crown. The first time He came, one star appeared in the East.

When He comes again, seated upon a white horse with his vestments stained in blood, the whole frame of nature will shake, the moon will drip blood and the sun will become as black as sackcloth.

On that glad day and in that victorious moment, the victim of the cross will become the victor of His kingdom. The prophecy of the angel shall come to pass:

> He shall be great, and shall be called the Son of the Highest: and the Lord God shall give unto him the throne of his father David: And he shall reign over the house of Jacob for ever; and of his kingdom there shall be no end (Luke 1:32, 33).

Then shall be fulfilled in totality the prophecy of Isaiah:

> For unto us a child is born, unto us a son is given: and the government shall be upon his shoulder: and his name shall be called Wonderful, Counsellor, The mighty God, The everlasting Father, The Prince of Peace. Of the increase of his government and peace there shall be no end, upon the throne of David, and upon his kingdom, to order it, and to establish it with judgment and with justice from henceforth even for ever (Isaiah 9:6, 7).

That will be, truly, a grand and glorious moment.

Millennial Reign

In the Bible, the Kingdom of Christ upon earth, this age of righteousness, is called a thousand-year reign. It means, in contemporary language, the millennial reign.

In the Book of Revelation, John mentions this thousand-year reign six times. But what about Satan?

The Bible says,

> And I saw an angel come down from heaven, hav-
> ing the key of the bottomless pit and a great chain
> in his hand. And he laid hold on the dragon, that
> old serpent, which is the Devil, and Satan, and
> bound him a thousand years. And cast him into the
> bottomless pit, and shut him up, and set a seal
> upon him, that he should deceive the nations no
> more, till the thousand years should be fulfilled
> (Revelation 20:1-3).

This is the rightful place for Satan, for he is Apollyon,
the king of the pit. There he will be confined with the millions of demons, fallen angels, the False Prophet and the
Antichrist for one thousand years. Satan's absence from the
earth will mean the absence of temptation, for the Bible
calls him "the tempter." The cause of sin will be bound and,
therefore, lawlessness will be easily controlled.

Then will be the glorious era when the righteous shall
take the reins of the government. What a day that will be!
The writer of Proverbs knew, "When the righteous are in
authority, the people rejoice" (29:2).

God's children, the saints who will return with Him to
earth, will rule the nations with Christ. This is His promises
to all who are overcomers in the power of His name:

> And he that overcometh, and keepeth my works unto
> the end, to him will I give power over the nations:
> And he shall rule them with a rod of iron; as the ves-
> sels of a potter shall they be broken to shivers: even
> as I received of my Father (Revelation 2:26, 27).

The faithful saints will be given authority over cities, just as promised by the Lord. "And he said unto him, Well, thou good servant: because thou hast been faithful in a very little, have thou authority over ten cities" (Luke 19:17). It is a glorious thought that some who were counted as insignificant by the men of this world might be placed as the mayor of the city in which they lived, for God will reward every man according to his works.

Daniel prophesied, "But the saints of the most High shall take the kingdom, and possess the kingdom for ever, even for ever and ever" (Daniel 7:18). He went on to say, "Until the Ancient of days came, and judgment was given to the saints of the most High; and the time came that the saints possessed the kingdom" (v. 22).

The apostle Paul reminded us of that coming kingdom and our privilege to reign with Christ, "If we suffer, we shall also reign with him" (2 Timothy 2:12).

Hallelujah! Even so come quickly, Lord Jesus!

This millennial kingdom will be characterized by peace. There will be no need for summit conferences or treaty organizations. Isaac Watts' hymn says:

> Jesus shall reign where'er the sun
> Doth His successive journeys run;
> His kingdom stretch from shore to shore,
> Till moons shall wax and wane no more.

The Bible says, "In his days shall the righteous flourish; and abundance of peace so long as the moon endureth" (Psalm 72:7). For the first time since man fell in the Garden of Eden, peace will truly reign. The promise of the angels will be fulfilled perfect and totally, "On earth, peace good will toward men" (Luke 2:14).

Today, all about us there are wars and rumors of wars. Kingdoms rise against kingdoms, nations against nations. But in that day, God will call upon people to make their weapons of war into agricultural implements:

> And he shall judge among the nations, and shall rebuke many people: and they shall beat their swords into plowshares, and their spears into pruninghooks: nation shall not lift up sword against nation, neither shall they learn war any more (Isaiah 2:4).

There will be complete disarmament without fear, for there will be no need for missiles, fighter jets, warheads or smart bombs: "And there shall be no more utter destruction; but Jerusalem shall be safely inhabited" (Zechariah 14:11).

A great change will also take place in the animal kingdom. Carnivorous, meat-eating animals will eat straw like the ox. Wild beasts will no longer prey one upon the other. A little child shall lead a lion. The leopard shall lie down with the kid and the young lion and the lamb shall dwell together. The cow and the bear shall feed side by side, and their young ones shall lie down together.

Here are the words of God from the Bible: "They shall not hurt nor destroy in all my holy mountain: for the earth shall be full of the knowledge of the Lord, as the waters cover the sea" (Isaiah 11:9).

What a glorious transformation!

Today millions suffer from lack of food; however, during the Millennial Kingdom, according to the Word of God, the land that was desolate will be like the Garden of Eden. In Isaiah's words, "The desert shall rejoice, and blossom as the rose" (35:1). "Israel shall blossom and bud, and fill the face of the world with fruit" (27:6).

The prophet Amos said the land shall be made so fertile, "The plowman shall overtake the reaper, and the treader of grapes him that soweth seed; and the mountains shall drop sweet wine, and all the hills shall melt" (9:13).

Prosperity will reign the world over. Every man will own his own home. Taxes will never come due. They shall not labor in vain, nor bring forth for trouble and long life shall be restored.

The patriarchs lived for hundreds of years. I believe this because the Bible tells us, but it also makes sense in light of modern medical science and what we now know about disease and weaknesses being passed from one generation to the next. In the early years of the human race, there were no genetic defects. These came gradually to human existence, as did the development of diseases and germs to prey upon human flesh. Thus, as time went on the entire human race carried with it and passed along to its offspring more and more illnesses and weakness, until life span grew shorter and shorter. Only with the advent of modern medicine and with the increase of knowledge in biological sciences has the life span of man begun to lengthen. For example, at the turn of the century the average life span in the United States was 49; today it is over 70 and lengthening to where more and more live past 100.

Think what the Millennium will bring. With Satan bound and sin under control, longevity will return. During that time, if one should happen to die at one hundred years of age, it will be viewed as the death of a child.

There will be a great revival of healing. The lame shall leap like a deer and the tongue of the dumb shall sing.

There will be no need for hospitals, doctors or asylums; no worry about insurance and sick benefits, and no need for convalescent homes.

The glory of the Lord will cover the earth. Holiness and righteousness will replace wickedness and evil. The high and lofty One—He that inhabiteth eternity, whose name is Holy—will rule in keeping with His perfect nature. All of the world will acknowledge Him, honor Him, and bow at His feet. All will acclaim Him King of Kings and Lord of Lords, and all nations will be subservient to, and send up praise to, His throne.

Just as the song puts it:

All hail the power of Jesus' name,
Let angels prostrate fall;
Bring forth the royal diadem,
And crown Him Lord of all.

Even the streets and highways of this new earthly kingdom will have holy names. Isaiah prophesied, "And an highway shall be there, and a way, and it shall be called The way of holiness" (Isaiah 35:8).

If you plan to live in this coming peaceful kingdom, you must have an experience of holiness with the Lord. The Bible says,

"Follow peace with all men, and holiness, without which no man shall see the Lord" (Hebrews 12:14).

"In that day shall there be upon the bells of the horses, HOLINESS UNTO THE LORD; and the pots in the Lord's house shall be like the bowls before the altar. Yea, every pot in Jerusalem and in Judah shall be holiness unto the Lord of hosts" (Zechariah 14:20, 21).

The bridles of the horses will bear the brand name "Holiness Unto The Lord." The bells of the bridles shall ring "Holiness Unto The Lord," and the redeemed shall say "Holiness Unto The Lord." In this holiness domain there will be no filth factories of pornography, neither violence, nor vandalism. There will be no taverns and no alcoholics. The righteous shall be in full authority.

The future is a bright and glorious prospect for those who will trust in the Lord Jesus Christ. One day this old world, as it presently exists, will go up in flames. The earth and all the works therein shall be burned up. But those who do the will of God shall abide forever and shall dwell in righteousness with Jesus Christ as King.

What a glorious and marvelous day that will be!

Conclusion

Over the years I have heard people speak rather disparagingly of Christian believers whom they say, are "Too heavenly-minded to be any earthly good." Atheistic Communism built its philosophy upon the idea that "Religion is the opiate of the people," implying that Christian believers are "stoned" and somewhat out of touch with reality. Even some sociologists today, as well as the secular media, speak or write disdainfully of a life of faith, hinting that Christian values, morals, and expectations are things not to be taken seriously by men and women of intelligence and sophistication.

If they only knew! If they could only for a moment grasp the truth and the reality of the living Christ! If they could only understand that the Bible is God's revelation of what is to come!

For 2,000 years now, men and women have tried to refute, to tear down and to prove false the Word of God. All such efforts have failed. Some of the most brilliant minds who set forth to prove the claims of Christ wrong ended up becoming staunch and faithful followers.

Where are you, today, in your search for faith? Have you met the Lord Jesus Christ? Have you been willing to bow a knee to Him, in faith believing that on a future day all knees will bow and all tongues will confess that He is Lord (Romans 14:11).

If no, I invite you to do so now.

Let us pray.

> *We rejoice, Oh heavenly Father, that even now we are citizens of another world, joint heirs with Christ to a future and glorious Kingdom. Let the truths of this message burn into readers' hearts. Draw them through Your Spirit to repentance and hope. Let them join us expectantly, as we wait in faith, for the unveiling of Your glory, the soon coming of Your kingdom. We pray in Jesus' name. Amen.*

And I saw a new heaven and a new earth:
for the first heaven and the first earth were
passed away; and there was no more sea.
And I John saw the holy city, new Jerusalem,
coming down from God out of heaven,
prepared as a bride adorned for her husband.
And I heard a great voice out of heaven
saying, Behold, the tabernacle of God is
with men, and he will dwell with them,
and they shall be his people, and God himself
shall be with them, and be their God.
And God shall wipe away all tears from their
eyes; and there shall be no more death,
neither sorrow, nor crying, neither shall
there be any more pain: for the former
things are passed away. And he that sat
upon the throne said, "Behold,
I make all things new"
(Revelation 21:1-5).

13

All Things Made New

Introduction

God's Word tells us John was in the Spirit on the Lord's day. While he was caught away in the Spirit, God pulled back the veil of heaven and allowed him to behold the glory of the new heaven and the new earth. John described his vision with graphic words which, over the years, have become common to Christian vocabulary. He speaks of:

- new heaven
- new earth
- holy city
- new Jerusalem
- a bride adorned for her husband
- the tabernacle of God
- no more death
- no more sorrow
- no more crying
- no more pain

These are the themes we sing, the assurances we

pass along to our children, the grand promises that gladden our hearts and brighten our path even when we walk down dark and stormy ways. These are the essentials of faith which both characterize and distinguish us from worldlings who have no hope.

The Old Order

Not just in the Book of Revelation but all through the Word we are reminded that this present heaven and earth shall pass away. Jesus noted that the divine words He uttered were more lasting than present creation "Heaven and earth shall pass away, but my words shall not pass away" (Matthew 24:35). His words must have still rung in the heart of his apostle, John, when he wrote many years later, "And the world passeth away, and the lust thereof: but he that doeth the will of God abideth for ever" (1 John 2:17).

The apostle Peter reminds us to keep life in perspective, realizing the transitory nature of both the creature (ourselves) and the creation (heaven and earth) and that ultimately we are all going to face God's judgment. "But the day of the Lord will come as a thief in the night; in the which the heavens shall pass away with a great noise, and the elements shall melt with fervent heat, the earth also and the works that are therein shall be burned up" (2 Peter 3:10). Peter goes on to say, "Nevertheless we, according to his promise, look for new heavens and a new earth, wherein dwelleth righteousness" (v. 13).

According to God's Word, this present heaven and earth will be destroyed and God will create a new heaven and a new earth. There is some controversy or question among theologians as to how this will be brought about. Some feel there will merely be a purification of the earth, a sort of cleansing as by fire, but I have no problem with the concept of a totally new heaven and new earth. Notice the terminology used by Isaiah the prophet, "For, behold, I create new heavens and a new earth: and the former shall not be remembered, nor come into mind" (Isaiah 65:17).

It must be remembered that He who created this heaven and earth is the creator of countless planets larger than this earth. It will be no task for Him to create a new heaven and a new earth for the saints of God to inhabit. Job said,

> He stretcheth out the north over the empty place, and hangeth the earth upon nothing. He bindeth up the waters in his thick clouds; and the cloud is not rent under them. He holdeth back the face of his throne, and spreadeth his cloud upon it. He hath compassed the waters with bounds, until the day and night come to an end. The pillars of heaven tremble and are astonished at his reproof. He divideth the sea with his power, and by his understanding he smiteth through the proud. By his spirit he hath garnished the heavens (26:7-13).

John also reminds us specifically that, "The former things are passed away" (Revelation 21:4). All those things that blighted the paradise of earth shall no longer exist. There shall be no more tears of sorrow; no more crying or death; no more pain or sickness. The absence of these things that have plagued the earth will be one of the greatest glories of heaven. The sin that robbed earth of its glory and brought about the curse will no longer exist.

Sin brought about a curse not only to humanity but also to all of God's creation. "Cursed is the ground for thy sake; in sorrow shalt thou eat of it all the days of thy life; Thorns also and thistles shall it bring forth to thee" (Genesis 3:17, 18). Paul tells us, "We know that the whole creation groaneth and travaileth in pain together until now" (Romans 8:22).

The whole of God's creation lives under the curse that sin has brought upon this world. The beauty of the flower is attacked by microscopic organisms that bring it to its death. Death entered into the world because of the curse of sin; and man, even from his birth, is a dying creature.

The New Order

But when God creates a new heaven and a new earth, flowers will bloom with the freshness of a thousand springtimes, replacing the thorns and thistles of earth. Mankind will have activity without fatigue in a land where flowers are perennial, where spring never fades, where night never comes, where pain is never felt, where sorrow never saddens and where tears never dim the eyes. In that new order, disappointment will never be known.

The other side, no curses there to blight
The robes those blessed ones wear,
made white in Jesus' blood.
No cry of grief, no voice of woe
to mar the peace that spirits know,
that constant peace with God.

The groans of this earth will be replaced with eternal singing. The barren landscape of this sin-struck earth will smile. Every vestige of curse will be destroyed, replaced with eternal blessing—the blessing that maketh rich and addeth no sorrow. What an exchange! A cursed earth for a blessed earth!

All Things New

As John beheld the new heaven and the new earth descending from God, he heard the voice of Him that sat upon the throne saying, "Behold, I make all things new" (Revelation 21:5).

What a thrill it must have been for John to know God was making special preparation for all His saints! Surely he remembered the Lord's own words who, just before leaving His sorrowing disciples, had said, "In my Father's house are many mansions: if it were not so, I would have told you. I go to prepare a place for you" (John 14:2).

This is the fountainhead of our hope and faith as well. Jesus is now making preparation for all believers.

Notice that in his vision John said, "I John saw the holy city, new Jerusalem, coming down from God out of heaven, prepared as a bride adorned for her husband" (Revelation 21:2). God is preparing this New Jerusalem as the capital city of the new heaven and new earth. That city will have splendor beyond compare.

The word *prepare* is used a number of times in the Scriptures with reference to the relationship God has with His church. Notice these statements:

"I go to prepare a place for you" (John 14:2).

"Eye hath not seen, nor ear heard, neither have entered into the heart of man, the things which God hath prepared for them that love Him" (1 Corinthians 2:9).

"[New Jerusalem] prepared as a bride adorned for her husband" (Revelation 21:2).

"But now they desire a better country, that is, an heavenly: wherefore God is not ashamed to be called their God: for he hath prepared for them a city" (Hebrews 11:16).

The splendors of all earthly cities pale before the majesty and glory of the New Jerusalem. That beauty beheld by John defies all earthly description.

This New Jerusalem is the city of promise mentioned all through the Bible. It is the goal toward which Abraham journeyed in faith: "For he looked for a city which hath foundations, whose builder and maker is God" (v. 10). No wonder Abraham lived by faith and was called "the father of the faithful," for he lived with the light of the city in his eyes; the things of this world strangely dim in comparison.

This is the true secret to all Christian living. If we can get a vision of the light that is to come, it guides our feet through the wilderness of life and lands us safely on the shores of sweet deliverance.

By faith Abraham could see that city. God had revealed to him there *was* such a city. Although Abraham was a wandering herdsman, not comfortable with cities, he knew there was a city whose architect and builder was God and he never lost his dream and his vision.

When I look up at night and see the sparkling stars and planets in a jet-black sky, I see the handiwork of God, declaring His glory. When I see the fleecy clouds wafting on the wind, with an azure blue backdrop, I see the glory of God. When I behold a golden sunset, with shafts of light beaming through the clouds—sometimes with every hue of the rainbow—I'm aware of the glory of God. When I look upon the oceans, the seas, the lakes, the rivers, the babbling brooks, I see the glory of God. When I stand before lofty mountains, looking out over the beautiful greenery of the earth, with more hues and shadows than can be counted, then I see the glory of God.

When I smell the fragrance of the rose, touch the petal of the lily, caress the wax-like splendor of the tulip, then I get a clear vision of the designs and ability of the master architect Who is personally preparing "the continuing city" (13:14) for His saints.

The New Jerusalem

Many of the treasures for which people search—sometimes amassing and then more often watching them slip through their fingers—will be commonplace in the city of God.

Gold will be used for pavement in that city. This will not be ordinary gold, but pure gold, as if it were transparent glass. And diamonds—which people guard with their lives—will be used as building material for the walls around the city.

The Bible tells us the walls of New Jerusalem will be 216 feet high and 6,000 miles around, for the city will be built as a square, 1500 miles on each of four sides. Precious stones that cause the heart of poor, earth-bound mortals to fill with greed shall be the material for the foundations of that walled city.

Unlike any wall this earth has ever known, this wall shall have twelve foundations, garnished with all manner of precious stones. The foundations shall be a blaze of color scintillating in the light of the Son of Righteousness, and reflecting a cataract of color like no artist could ever portray. Beauty beyond description!

God's New Jerusalem, our city of promise, will have twelve gates, three to a side, each made of a single, solid pearl.

Imagine, those things so scarce and precious on this present earth—all those things for which men have striven and fought—will be commonplace in New Jerusalem. Why then should any saint of God really fret over the burdens of this life? After this fleeting journey is through, everything for which the heart can wish is just waiting, "Reserved in heaven for you, Who are kept by the power of God through faith unto salvation ready to be revealed in the last time" (1 Peter 1:4, 5).

In that new city, every dwelling place is a golden mansion, every step is filled with triumph, every headpiece is a crown. In that city food is plentiful and served banquet style. Every day is a rapture, every hour is jubilee, every moment is filled with glory.

Every believer's mansion will be glorious, with the glory of the Son of Righteousness reflecting the beauty of the multicolored foundations of the city.

What a prospect for the child of God! What a city in which to live—a city filled with saints! What a blessed fellowship! A city where God heads the government— holy rule! A city where God lives and the saints of God shall dwell. This is the preparation God is making for every man and woman who will live for Him.

Conclusion

Think about it. Does not such news make you yearn for heaven? Does it not put life into a different perspective? Does it not entice you? Does it not make you want to be freed from the powers of this sin-cursed earth?

I implore you now, on the premise that God has prepared indescribable raptures for those who will accept His Son, to make your calling and election sure. Your life on this earth, at best, is but a short span. What you can enjoy or gain of this present world's pleasures is but infinitesimal, or immeasurably small, when compared to the glories that await the redeemed for all eternity.

Are you a Christian? If not, then seek Him now.

Let us pray.

> *Father in heaven, Creator of all, giver of life, lover of the oppressed, come near us this moment and make Your presence felt. Open our hearts to feel You, open our eyes to see You, open our ears to hear You. And lead us to the Way, the Truth and the Life embodied in the person of Your only begotten Son. We recognize Him only as our hope. We turn to Him only as our Savior. And we place our trust now and for all time and eternity in Him and His redemption. In the name of Jesus we pray. Amen.*

*And I saw a great white throne, and him that
sat on it, from whose face the earth and the
heaven fled away; and there was found no place
for them. And I saw the dead, small and
great, stand before God; and the books
were opened: and another book was opened,
which is the book of life: and the dead were
judged out of those things
which were writtenin the books*
(Revelation 20:11, 12).

14

The Great White Throne Judgment

Introduction

It is a sobering fact that all of us must come to judgment. And we must be judged for all our deeds, both secret and public. Regardless of our station in life, or status, we must all stand in judgment before God our Creator.

While not a pleasant thought, it is a rational thought. Our very concept of God incorporates His divine characteristics of justice and immutability. Such terms in reference to the character of God make it impossible for any sin or any evil to go unpunished.

In today's society, justice may fail. It never fails with God. The human judge may make a mistake, he may not have all the facts; but God has all the facts, God understands all the circumstances, and God never makes a mistake. In God's court, perfect justice always prevails.

Not only does this concept parallel the rational feelings of the human heart—our inner knowledge that those who do wrong should have to pay for it—but it is declared to be truth in the Bible, God's Word itself. The writer of Hebrews tells us, "It is appointed unto men once to die, but after this the judgment" (Hebrews 9:27).

Paul stated it even more succinctly when summing up his sermon on Mars Hill by stating, "Because he hath appointed a day, in the which he will judge the world in righteousness by that man whom he hath ordained; whereof he hath given assurance unto all men, in that he hath raised him from the dead" (Acts 17:31).

This fact of judgment being true, let us note some of the things God's Word tells us about judgment.

Judgment of the Cross

Let us look first at the judgment of the Cross. It was there, at the cross of the Lord Jesus Christ, where judgment was passed upon sin.

The heart of the Christian message is embodied in the golden text of the Bible: "For God so loved the world, that he gave his only begotten Son, that whosoever believeth in him should not perish, but have everlasting life" (John 3:16). We understand the full extent of God's loving and God's giving at Calvary, where He permitted His Son to die in our place.

All sin was judged at the Cross.

When we come to the Cross, when we bow at the Cross—believing in Christ and accepting Him as Savior and Lord—then all our sins are washed away. They have been judged, placed upon Christ and forever removed. We will never face those sins again. The Word of God tells us they have gone before to judgment: "Some men's sins are open beforehand, going before to judgment; and some men they follow after" (1 Timothy 5:24).

Other Scripture references include God's promise to Israel through the prophet Isaiah: "I have blotted out, as a thick cloud, thy transgressions, and, as a cloud, thy sins: return unto me; for I have redeemed thee" (Isaiah 44:22); His promise through Micah: "He will have compassion upon us; he will subdue our iniquities; and . . . wilt cast all [our] sins into the depths of the sea" (Micah 7:19); and God's New Testament promise through Peter following the healing of the lame man: "Repent ye therefore, and be converted, that your sins may be blotted out" (Acts 3:19).

By kneeling at the cross of Christ, we can have judgment passed upon all our sins now. Our sins will be cast into the depths of the sea. They will be blotted out. We will never have to face them again.

This is the judgment of the Cross.

Judgment of Rewards

There is also a judgment of rewards which will take place when Jesus comes for His church. At this judgment, Christians will be judged according to their works. This judgment will be conducted in the great audience chamber of heaven before the Judgment Seat of Christ.

All Christians must face judgment. Paul tells us,

Every one of us shall give account of himself to God (Romans 14:12).

For we must all appear before the judgment seat of Christ; that every one may receive the things done in his body, according to that he hath done, whether it be good or bad (2 Corinthians 5:10)

Now if any man build upon this foundation gold, silver, precious stones, wood, hay, stubble; Every man's work shall be made manifest: for the day shall declare it, because it shall be revealed by fire; and the fire shall try every man's work of what sort it is. If any man's work abide which he hath built thereupon, he shall receive a reward (1 Corinthians 3:12-14).

For the Christian, this is not a judgment that will determine eternal life or admittance to heaven. Heaven is not earned by works, but through grace by faith in Christ's shed blood. This will be a judgment of rewards for the labors of God's children. That is when we, the saints, will be rewarded according to our faithfulness and our service in the kingdom of God and His church.

That is when the Lord's perfect knowledge of things will be revealed. There will be some surprises when those who appeared least among us are revealed as greatest (See Luke 9:48). The Lord clearly promised, "Love ye your enemies, and do good, and lend, hoping for nothing again; and your reward shall be great" (Luke 6:35): just as He noted those who suffer and are persecuted in this life will be more than compensated in the life to come. "Blessed are ye, when men shall revile you, and persecute you, and

shall say all manner of evil against you falsely, for my
sake. Rejoice, and be exceeding glad: for great is your
reward in heaven" (Matthew 5:11, 12).

Judgment of Nations

There is also to be a judgment of the nations. This
judgment will take place on earth when the Lord comes
in power and great glory. It will be conducted before He
establishes His millennial kingdom upon earth.

All nations will be called before Him and Jesus Christ
will judge them according to their treatment of the Jews.
This judgment will result in the division of what the Bible
calls the "sheep and the goats." Some will be saved for the
earthly kingdom and will reign with Christ for a thousand
years. Others will be consigned to everlasting fire.

God will purge out of His Kingdom all things that
offend and them which do iniquity. His millennial reign
on this earth will not be disturbed by the hard-hearted,
unrepentant, goat nations; but all will be peace.

We have a glimpse of this in the passage,

> Then shall he answer them, saying, Verily I say
> unto you, Inasmuch as ye did it not to one of the
> least of these, ye did it not to me. And these shall
> go away into everlasting punishment: but the
> righteous into life eternal (Matthew 25:45, 46).

The Great White Throne Judgment

The final judgment is called the Great White Throne
Judgment. This judgment will take place at the end of the

Millennial Reign. It will be conducted by the Judge of all men, seated upon a sparkling white throne, whose glory is so magnificent and so great that heaven and earth shall both flee away.

Evidently, the Scripture means the heavens above us, which we can now behold with our natural eyes, and the earth will take their flight. The Great White Throne Judgment will be conducted in the dwelling place of God, which is called in the Bible the heaven that is high above all heavens.

Someone will rationalize that this is an impossibility, but we must remember this Judge who sits upon the throne is the Creator of the heaven and the earth. The wind is in His fists. He rides upon the wings of the wind. He makes the clouds His chariots and the beams of His chambers are in the waters. This is He who meted out the heaven with a span, weighed the hills in a balance and the mountains in scales. All things are possible with God.

In my opinion, the earth will flee away because it was the scene of man's sin where Christ was driven to Calvary to shed His blood. The heavens will flee away—that is, the atmospheric heaven—because it is the dwelling place of Satan, the prince of the power of the air.

For those holding on to the world and making this world their portion, remember the Scripture, "And the world passeth away, and the lust thereof: but he that doeth the will of God abideth for ever" (1 John 2:17). For those who have made the world their lot, when this judgment comes, all hope is gone.

The Great White Throne Judgment is not a general judgment where both the righteous and the wicked shall

THE GREAT WHITE THRONE JUDGMENT

stand before God; but it is a judgment of the wicked. "But the rest of the dead lived not again until the thousand years were finished. This is the first resurrection" (Revelation 20:5).

This will not be merely the throne of a king, but the throne of a judge. It will not be a governing throne but a throne for passing sentence. And the Judge's verdict will be one of eternal consequences.

The Wicked Judged

Who will be judged at the Great White Throne? The Bible leaves no doubt on this point:

> And I saw a great white throne, and him that sat on it, from whose face the earth and the heaven fled away; and there was found no place for them. And I saw the dead, small and great, stand before God; and the books were opened: and another book was opened, which is the book of life: and the dead were judged out of those things which were written in the books, according to their works. And the sea gave up the dead which were in it; and death and hell delivered up the dead which were in them: and they were judged every man according to their works. And death and hell were cast into the lake of fire. This is the second death. And whosoever was not found written in the book of life was cast into the lake of fire (Revelation 20:11-15).

According to our study of the former judgments, the righteous have already been judged. Therefore, only those lost ones, or the wicked, shall come before the Great White Throne.

Those who have died outside Christ will be held in confinement until the morning of judgment. Then their bodies shall be brought forth from the grave; and the spirit shall unite with the body and be brought to the Great White Throne Judgment. "And death and hell were cast into the lake of fire. This is the second death" (v. 14).

This is the Second Resurrection.

Second Resurrection

The Bible speaks of the resurrection of the just and the unjust:

> "And have hope toward God, which they themselves also allow, that there shall be a resurrection of the dead, both of the just and unjust" (Acts 24:15).

> "Many of them that sleep in the dust of the earth shall awake, some to everlasting life, and some to shame and everlasting contempt" (Daniel 12:2).

> "And shall come forth; they that have done good, unto the resurrection of life; and they that have done evil, unto the resurrection of damnation" (John 5:29).

> "But the rest of the dead lived not again until the thousand years were finished. This is the first resurrection. Blessed and holy is he that hath part in the first resurrection" (Revelation 20:5, 6).

The Second Resurrection, which is a resurrection of damnation and a resurrection unto shame and everlasting contempt, will take place at the time of the Great White Throne Judgment. That is when the sea shall give up its dead, and when death and hell shall deliver up their dead to stand in judgment before the Almighty.

The question may be asked: "If the righteous are not to be judged at this time, why does the Judge open the Book of Life?"

The Book of Life will be opened as a proof to those who are being judged that they are unworthy of eternal life. Their names are not written therein. "And whosoever was not found written in the book of life was cast into the lake of fire" (Revelation 20:15).

Believers can have assurance today that their names are in the Book of Life. Jesus said, "Rejoice, because your names are written in heaven" (Luke 10:20). It is better to have your name recorded on high than to have it recorded in every book of fame throughout the world. Job joyfully proclaimed, "My witness is in heaven, and my record is on high" (Job 16:19).

The purpose of this judgment is not to decide whether a person is saved or lost, because that decision is made before any of us dies. The Bible plainly states, "He that believeth and is baptized shall be saved; but he that believeth not shall be damned" (Mark 16:16); and again, "He that believeth not is condemned [or judged] already" (John 3:18).

Unless a sinner receives forgiveness from God, he is facing eternal judgment. The Great White Throne Judgment is the imposition of this death sentence to prove and show the justice of God and to vindicate the righteousness of God because men rejected the blood of His Son.

No one will be exempt from this judgment. The Scripture says, "I saw the dead, small and great, stand before God" (Revelation 20:12).

The Judge of all the earth is no respecter of persons and will not regard distinction. There will be no bribes, no appeals to higher courts. All judgment will be final. There will be no chance for rebuttal, no attorneys or advocates, no one to help.

Just as there are degrees of rewards for those who are saved, at this judgment there will be degrees of punishment also for those who are lost. The Bible speaks of some receiving greater damnation (Mark 12:40). And repeatedly, the terminology "more tolerable" is used. Thus, I believe there will be greater judgment for some than others.

Man shall not get away from his works, for the Bible says he will be judged according to his works. Man dies and leaves this world, but his works follow him. Unredeemed man not only leaves the mark and a slimy trail of sin behind him, but his sin follows him to the judgment. At the judgment, his sin will condemn him to the lake of fire. Hidden sins will be brought to light and full justice will be meted out. Not one sin that man has committed will go unpunished, "For the wages of sin is death" (Romans 6:23).

Second Death

Not only does sin bring about physical death, but it is certain to bring about the second death or hell.

Verification is found in God's Word, "Be sure your sin will find you out" (Numbers 32:23).

If sin does not find you out in this present life, it will be waiting on you at the Great White Throne Judgment. The Judge of all the earth, Who will sit upon the throne of purity with eyes as flames of fire, will look into the darkened recesses of your heart and reveal the wickedness of your soul. At the Great White Throne Judgment, the wicked will face their records and man will be without excuse.

The Great White Throne Judgment will not be a debate with God over right or wrong, but it will be a revelation of the evil of humanity and will show forth the justice of Almighty God and His anger against sin.

All pleas for pardon will be rejected for the man who was once the Savior will then be the Judge, and all verdicts must be "guilty."

No doubt, some will make the plea on the basis of their goodness and their noble deeds or benevolence. Some will make a plea on the premise of their righteousness. But Jesus has already said,

> Many will say to me in that day, Lord, Lord, have we not prophesied in thy name? and in thy name have cast out devils? and in thy name done many wonderful works? And then will I profess unto them, I never knew you: depart from me, ye that work iniquity (Matthew 7:22, 23).

Good deeds and good works will not stand the test at the judgment. Merely to be a reputable person and a respectable citizen is not enough. To belong to the church and to various civic societies is not enough. To be charitable and to give to the poor is not enough.

"For by grace are ye saved through faith; and that not of yourselves: it is the gift of God: Not of works, lest any man should boast" (Ephesians 2:8, 9).

Conclusion

To sum up these remarks, I would like to use two verses found in the Old Testament:

"And what will ye do in the day of visitation, and in the desolation which shall come from far? to whom will ye flee for help? and where will ye leave your glory" (Isaiah 10:3);

"What then shall I do when God riseth up? and when he visiteth, what shall I answer him?" (Job 31:14).

I leave these questions with you.

- What will you do in the day of visitation?
- To whom will you flee for help?
- Where will you leave your glory?
- What will you do when God rises up?
- What will you answer Him?

Now is your chance to make your decision for the Lord Jesus Christ. Tomorrow may be too late. Tomorrow, the tender, loving Savior will be your judge.

Today, Jesus Christ will pass judgment upon your sins and cast them into the depths of the sea. Tomorrow, God will pass judgment upon your sins, and cast you into the lake of fire. Which will you choose?

Let us pray.

Dear God in heaven, grant us mercy that is abundant, full and free, through Your son Jesus Christ. Open our eyes to see the coming judgment. Open our hearts to realize where we presently stand, without hope except through Your mercy. Accept our petitions for grace and our prayers for forgiveness, and make us righteous through the shed blood of your Son. We pray in His holy name. Amen.

And I saw a new heaven and a new earth: for the first heaven and the first earth were passed away; and there was no more sea. And I John saw the holy city, new Jerusalem, coming down from God out of heaven, prepared as a bride adorned for her husband (Revelation 21:1, 2).

15

Heaven— Capital City

Introduction

Just off the coast of Asia Minor about 24 miles out in the Aegean Sea is an isle called Patmos. It is a very significant place, because from this island a preacher viewed the splendor of the capital city of heaven. The Bible says that John was in the Spirit on the Lord's Day and through the Spirit he viewed the splendor, magnitude and glory of the city of God.

John describes his vision:

> And I saw a new heaven and a new earth: for the first heaven and the first earth were passed away; and there was no more sea. And I John saw the holy city, new Jerusalem, coming down from God out of heaven, prepared as a bride adorned for her husband (Revelation 21:1, 2).

The New Jerusalem was the capital city of heaven, called "the heavenly Jerusalem." In John's vision, the capital city of heaven became the capital city of the earth. This is the city Abraham sought when he left his home in Ur of the Chaldees: "For he looked for a city which hath foundations, whose builder and maker is God" (Hebrews 11:10). You will notice that the Word of God says the architect and builder of this city is God.

Kings and governments of earth have built their great cities. Some earthly cities have gained fame throughout the whole world. Rome, the city that sits upon seven hills, was once a world power and was even called "the Eternal City." Yet today, the glory of Rome has faded, leaving the ruins of the Coliseum and pillars of the temples that serve stark notice that Rome was not an eternal city.

Visit beautiful Paris on the Seine, see the Eiffel Tower, Notre Dame, and Arch of Triumph. Visit Venice, the queen of the Adriatic. Visit Washington with its domed Capitol and its Washington Monument towering hundreds of feet above the city. See the Jefferson Memorial and the magnificent White House. Visit New York City, the crossroads of North America, and notice the skyline with buildings towering into the air. Ascend 102 floors of the Empire State Building, marvel at its architecture, and muse over the importance of such a place in a complex world. Walk down Fifth Avenue during an Easter Parade and see the beauty and gaiety. All of these cities were made by human hands and shall one day fade like a leaf. Just as Babylon, Rome and other great cities of the past, these mighty cities will one day fall. "For here have we no continuing city, but we seek one to come" (Hebrews 13:14).

Eternal City

The New Jerusalem is to be an eternal city, especially

prepared for the saints of God. "But now they desire a better country, that is, an heavenly: wherefore God is not ashamed to be called their God: for he hath prepared for them a city" (Hebrews 11:16).

This was our Lord Jesus Christ's personal testimony while here on earth: "I go to prepare a place for you. And if I go and prepare a place for you, I will come again, and receive you unto myself; that where I am, there ye may be also" (John 14:2, 3).

All of the splendors of the earthly cities pale in light of the glory of the New Jerusalem. There is no comparison. God's Word describes this capital city.

Abraham testified he sought a city that had foundations; and, in his vision, John saw the foundations of the eternal city: "And the wall of the city had twelve foundations, and in them the names of the twelve apostles of the Lamb" (Revelation 21:14). John goes on to tell us, "The foundations of the wall of the city were garnished with all manner of precious stones" (Revelation 21:19).

Twelve Foundations

The first foundation was made of jasper, which is pure diamond.

The second foundation was made of sapphire, which is a beautiful blue.

The third foundation was made of chalcedony, which is sky blue.

The fourth foundation was made of emerald, which is green.

The fifth foundation was made of sardonyx, which is red and white.

The sixth foundation was made of sardius, which is fiery red.

The seventh was made of chrysolyte, which is golden.

The eighth was made of beryl, which is sea green.

The ninth was made of topaz, which is transparent green.

The 10th was made of chrysoprasus, which is purple.

The 11th was made of jacinth, which is orange.

The 12th was made of amethyst, which is violet.

What a magnificence of color! Resplendent beyond imagination! The foundations of the City of God shimmering, scintillating in the light of the Son of Righteousness.

Built on these sparkling foundations was a wall great and high. The Bible says, "And the building of the wall of it was jasper: and the city was pure gold, like unto clear glass" (Revelation 21:18). The height of the wall was 144 cubits or approximately 216 feet.

To use John's terminology, the city was built foursquare, 1500 miles on either side, which means that the perimeter was 6,000 miles, equal to a journey from the tip of Florida to the top of Maine, across to Billings, Montana; down to El Paso, Texas; and back around the Gulf of Mexico to Miami. Around this city is a beautiful wall made of jasper which is pure diamond.

I have been to the Kimberly Diamond Mines of South Africa and have seen beautiful and sparkling diamonds. I have seen the lengendary Koh-i-noor Diamond, among the British crown jewels. Today, the largest of diamonds known to man is two and one-half ounces, but the wall that will surround our mansions in glory will be one solid diamond, 216 feet high and 6,000 miles around.

Compare the largest diamond of earth with this, if you will, and it looks like a tallow candle in comparison with the sun. This sparkling diamond wall reflects the light of God's glory throughout the city and thousands of miles around.

Streets of Gold

The streets of this city, New Jerusalem, are not made of macadam, concrete or brick. They are gold. "And the street of the city was pure gold, as it were transparent glass" (Revelation 21:21).

Earthlings will grasp for gold and sell their souls for a paltry sum, but even the poorest of God's saints will walk upon highly refined gold throughout eternity. The floors of our mansions shall be transparent gold.

Twelve Gates

The capital city has twelve entrances, three gates on either side. These gates have angels to guard them and they are never closed night or day. "And the gates of it shall not be shut at all by day: for there shall be no night there" (Revelation 21:25).

The Portuguese government boasts of having a pearl bigger than a pear, but each of the gates in New Jerusalem will be one pearl. We do not know how large these gates are, but in order to admit the multitudes they would have to be mammoth.

Did you ever stop to think of how pearls come into existence? Pearls are made through suffering. In his book *The Triumph of the Crucified,* Erich Sauer explains it like

THE RAPTURE AND REVELATION

this: "It originates through specially strong secretion of mother of pearl, by the pearl shellfish as a reaction against injury from without. It is thus the answer of a wounded life to injury from without."

Likewise the gates of heaven were opened by suffering. We have access to the city only through the sufferings of Calvary; these pearly gates were made on Calvary.

Dimensions of the City

Now let us look more closely at the dimensions of this city. "And the city lieth foursquare, and the length is as large as the breadth: and he measured the city with the reed, twelve thousand furlongs. The length and the breadth and the height of it are equal" (Revelation 21:16).

The city is a perfect cube which, according to the calculations of some, is 512 quintillion cubic feet. According to William Biederwolf, if the world stood for 100,000 years and always had and always will have a billion people on it dying off every generation, that would make only 300 trillion people. He further said, "If that isn't big enough, God could send His surveying angels out and throw His boundary line around a few sextillion acres more."

To further show the magnitude of this city, I quote from the book *The Triumph of the Crucified*: "All the buildings in the world, all houses and all, all cities and villages, everything which the billions of people today inhabit taken together do not make 300 cubic miles. Thus there is room in the heavenly Jerusalem for hundreds of thousands of generations, and yet according to biblical chronology only 200 generations have passed since Adam."

We should just now begin to understand what Jesus meant when He said, "In my father's house are many mansions" (John 14:2). It is difficult for the finite mind to comprehend what God means by many, because we are so limited in our figures. One reason heaven has lost its charm for a lot of people is because they have tried to compare it with something earthly. There is nothing earthly that can be compared with the glory that shall be revealed. Think of a city where every home is a mansion, where Jesus is King, where angels are the attendants and where all citizens are saints.

My celestial home and my mansion in glory will be brilliant as the sunset. Instead of plastered walls, jasper walls; instead of highly polished hardwood floors, transparent golden floors; instead of any of the modern lighting systems, the Lamb will be the light.

What a thrill to know that my home will be lighted throughout eternity by the Bright and Morning Star and the Son of Righteousness! The Scripture says there will be no need for the sun, for the Lamb is the light thereof (Revelation 21:23). The Son of Righteousness will shine upon the multicolored foundations of the city of God and reflect the beauty into our mansions.

The water system in our mansion in glory will be clear as crystal, coming from beneath the throne of God and of the Lamb. It will not be water that needs to be filtered for it is the fountain of living water.

If you love river scenery, this city will intrigue you; for never a clearer, more sparkling, crystal-like water flowed in any river. On either side of this river of life there is the tree of life, bearing twelve manner of fruit, one fruit for every month of the year. This is the orchard of the city of God.

In that New Jerusalem there will be no slums or mediocre neighborhoods, for only the elite will live there. By the grace of God we all become the elite. The Word of God says, "Unto him that loved us, and washed us from our sins in his own blood, And hath made us kings and priests unto God and his Father" (Revelation 1:5, 6).

There shall be no cemeteries there—a city without grief or graves, without birth or burial, without tombs to constantly remind us of the enemy called death—for death can never knock on heaven's door.

There will be no need for a welfare agency, for all will be rich. There will be no need for a home for the aged, for this city is a land where we will never grow old. The river of life is the fountain of youth. The city directory is the book of life, for all of the citizens are saints. A city without discord or violence, the New Jerusalem will be the headquarters of harmony.

What a glorious thrill it will be to hear the song of Moses and the Lamb and the songs of the redeemed of all ages blending together in perfect harmony, accompanied by Gabriel's trumpet and David's harp! The grandeur of nature, the glory of art, the dreams of this earth and the creations of poetry all fade in this vision of glory.

Conclusion

Does not a place of such unspeakable splendor draw you—a place which is the home of our Father, the residence of His family and the hope of all ages?

If you long for such a place, it is possible for you to become a citizen of that eternal city even now. The Bible tells us, "Blessed are they that do his commandments, that they may have right to the tree of life, and may enter in through the gates into the city" (Revelation 22:14).

Through simple obedience to Christ, you can be made a fit subject for heaven. Jesus has purchased your redemption and is preparing a place in that city for you. He wants *all* to meet the conditions for admission: "Not willing that any should perish, but that all should come to repentance" (2 Peter 3:9). He is calling upon you today to repent, to believe, and to receive your inheritance in heaven.

Let us pray.

> *Father in heaven, in each human heart You have created a vacuum, an inner sanctum where we all yearn for paradise lost. Though we try to fill that void with many things, we fail miserably and end up altogether lonely, frustrated, tormented by guilt and unable to find our way out of darkness into light. Thank You for Jesus, Light of the World. Thank You for His message of love and forgiveness. And thank You for the promise He shares with us of eternal life in Your heavenly city, New Jerusalem. We give Him our allegiance. We proclaim Him as our Lord, through faith, and we place our present and eternal destiny in His hands. Amen.*